SYMBOLIC INDUCEMENT AND KNOWING

STUDIES IN RHETORIC / COMMUNICATION
Carroll C. Arnold, *Series Editor*

Symbolic Inducement and Knowing:
A STUDY IN THE FOUNDATIONS OF RHETORIC

By Richard B. Gregg

N *University of South Carolina Press*

First Edition

Published in Columbia, South Carolina, by the
University of South Carolina Press

Manufactured in the United States of America

Library of Congress Cataloging in Publication Data
Gregg, Richard B., 1936–
    Symbolic inducement and knowing.
    (Studies in rhetoric/communication)
    Bibliography: p.
    Includes index.
    1. Symbolism in communication. 2. Languages—Philosophy.
3. Knowledge, Theory of. 4. Symbolic interactionism.
5. Rhetoric. I. Title. II. Series.
P91.G7 1984   808'.001   83-26113
ISBN 0-87249-434-9

CONTENTS

FOREWORD

With this book the University of South Carolina Press inaugurates a series of volumes treating rhetoric and general communication. *Symbolic Inducement and Knowing* deals with a fundamental question about humans as communicative beings: Do we "know" because we perceive what is outside our skins as "stars," "decibels," "sweet and sour," "fragrant or malodorous," "soft or hard," or do we "know" the universe in direct symbol-less ways and then invent symbols by which to express our knowledge? Richard Gregg undertakes to synthesize the claims that can be made for affirming the first of these two assertions. He explores the supports for and the implications of saying that humans belong to a peculiarly symbol-using, symbol-making, and symbol-misusing species.

To develop his argument Gregg draws on anthropological, neurophysiological, psycholinguistic, psychological, literary, and rhetorical theories and findings. He presents an eclectic, comprehensive analysis of evidence suggesting what it means to say that humans are symbolizers, essentially. Gregg does not simply assert the existence of symbolic behaviors, as many have done; he studies symbolic behavior as interaction with external environment. In doing so he brings up to date a historic line of argument that has gained new prominence during the last half-century.

The viewpoint Gregg espouses is not, of course, without competitors. Idealist alternatives have been offered at least since the time of Plato. Idealists typically claim that the human mind can know "realities" that are beyond the reach of the senses. Mind is superior to and distinct from body, it is said. Ideas are more "real" than matter. Intuition, aided by disciplined thought or faith, can apprehend Platonic Forms, divine truths, or other transcendent "realities." Symbolic systems are arbitrarily devised codes, constructed as convenient, instrumental means of re-presenting the transcendently known. Justification for using such systems is measured by expression's faithfulness to the realities of properly formed ideas. The contingent and idiosyncratic tend to be deplored by idealists, and discourse about the contingent is disvalued. Thus the exclusion of poets and rhetoricians from Plato's republic and St. Augustine's depreciation of discourse about "sensible things."

Cartesian points of view have much in common with idealistic views. Cartesian positions stress separation of mind from body; they posit existence of self-evident ideas intuitively recognized; and they define symbolic systems as arbitrary codes—as convenient instrumentalities—to be judged for the accuracy with which they represent the known. As Samuel Ijessling has pointed out in his *Rhetoric and Philosophy in Conflict,* the historical result of Cartesian-positivistic philosophies has been that, "How a text really takes shape, what exactly happens whenever a text is written or read, what a text effects in the reader or listener, are questions which are not raised" (p. 68). Naked truth and bare facts have first rank; all else that humans symbolize is play at best and delusion at worst. To induce perceptions or beliefs symbolically is considered by Cartesians and positivists dangerous and deceptive.

Another analysis less at odds with the symbolic-action theory explored by Gregg is commonly traced to David Hume and other British empiricists. This viewpoint asserts that knowledge originates in sensory data. Impressions or other representations of sensory experience are stored and lawfully associated in the mind. Once more, it is asserted that symbolic systems are arbitrarily conceived and are rendered conventional and convenient through use. They are, it is said, products of innate human capacities to label, associate, abstract, and thereby to invent signs and symbols. Once created, symbolic systems can have psychological and cultural influences, but this is the consequence of the systems' structural characteristics and their representational potentialities. Generally speaking, empiricist theories of man posit that states of feeling are the progenitors of reason. Knowing is thus fundamentally experiential and only secondarily the product of "rational" processes originating in the mind.

Behaviorism extends empiricism to turn idealism on its head. Not mind, but body, is "reality." Humans are complex, conditionable animals, different from other animals in no fundamental ways. Knowledge is the product of stimuli experienced and responded to; it is the bit-by-bit accumulation of experience, possessed by the physiological system. Symbolic systems are arbitrarily created codes, learned through social conditioning. Thought is bodily activity, sometimes verbal, sometimes visceral, sometimes manual. All complex behaviors are integrations of established stimulus-response connections. Communication is calculated stimulation of other conditioned organisms.

The analysis of symbolization, knowing, and communicating that Gregg sets forth borrows from both empiricist and behaviorist traditions, but its important deviation from those systems of thought lies in its denial that symbolic systems are arbitrary. It asserts that symbolization is *the* characteristically human way of perceiving, processing, possessing, and expressing knowledge. This claim is not new, though its prominence in

viii

Western philosophy, psychology, and theory of literary and rhetorical communication has risen anew in the twentieth century.

A form of symbolic-action analysis can be traced to pre-Socratic Greece, most specifically to Gorgias of Leontini who lived in the fifth century B.C. Gorgias asserted that humans know through their senses but can possess sensory knowledge only symbolically. Accordingly, one cannot say a human *knows* external "reality," for the senses can deceive; moreover, much of what is learned sensorily is never possessed in the forms of communicative symbols. It is impossible to say all that one knows; and if one could say all one knows, no one else could experience the identical thought, feeling, or image that gave rise to the symbols used in expression. Precise, accurate communication is thus impossible, thought Gorgias; a kind of "illusion" or "deception" informs all experience and all communication. The fullest and best use of symbolic activity is to display the varied splendors of the human mind.

For most of the twenty-five centuries since Gorgias, his interpretation of knowing as essentially symbolic has been overshadowed by idealist, Cartesian, and exclusively empirical views. To a significant degree Gregg's exploration in *Symbolizing and Knowing* is an inventory of how far modern scientific and philosophical research and theory can refine and give flesh to an essentially Gorgianic vision of life as symbolic experience.

Gregg's position has its contemporary roots in twentieth-century philosophy, theory of art, and literary theory, though the beginnings of symbolic-action theory are frequently traced to Johann von Herder's *Outlines of the Philosophy of Man* (1784–1791) and to European philosophers interested in expanding aspects of Kant's philosophical system. In the United States, however, symbolic-action theory derives most directly from writings by Ernst Cassirer, Suzanne K. Langer, and Kenneth Burke.

Cassirer's anthropologically based theory of symbolic action appeared first in his three-volume *Philosophy of Symbolic Forms,* published in German between 1923 and 1929 and in English in 1957. Admitting her deep indebtedness to Cassirer, Suzanne Langer issued her *Philosophy in a New Key* in 1942 and her *Mind: An Essay on Human Feeling* (2 volumes) in 1967. In these works Langer heralded *symbolic transformation* as the "new key" that "alters our concept of intelligence at a stroke" (*Philosophy in a New Key,* p. 33).

The voluminous writings of Kenneth Burke interpret literature and rhetoric as symbolic action, and they have therefore drawn special attention from other twentieth-century literary and rhetorical scholars in this country. Burke's *The Philosophy of Literary Form* (1941), *A Rhetoric of Motives* (1950), and *Language as Symbolic Action* (1966) stand out as seminal works. Where in later studies Cassirer focused on the role of symbolic action in historical epochs and Langer explored symbolic action in the history of art, Burke's steady insistence that literary and pragmatic communication are *inducing* symbolic actions has strongly influenced American students of rhetoric. It is from this Burkean emphasis that Richard Gregg proceeds in his quest for understanding of what *symbolic inducement* can mean physiologically, linguistically, socially, and as a basis for criticism of rhetoric. The exposition he has produced is the most comprehensive that has been offered since Langer's *Mind: An Essay on Human Feeling.*

Carroll C. Arnold
Editor, *Rhetoric/Communication*
University of South Carolina Press

ACKNOWLEDGMENTS

While preparing this book, I incurred debts to a number of colleagues, students, and friends who helped to guide my research, evaluated my work, assisted in preparation of the manuscript and gave general encouragement.

For substantive contributions and expert criticism I want to express special thanks to Kathy Harbert, Nancy Dunbar, Walter B. Weimer, and Carroll C. Arnold, all of whom provided suggestions concerning content and presentation as the work progressed. For evaluating my interpretations of physiological and psychological data I thank the following members of the Department of Psychology at The Pennsylvania State University: Thomas D. Borkovec, Michael J. Mahoney, and, again, Walter B. Weimer. For advice of quite a different sort, I am indebted to James M. Cartey, Manager for Architectural Structural Planning and Design at Penn State. It was he who helped me to understand the rhetorical features of architecture and interior design. The following colleagues in the Department of Speech Communication at Penn State gave my work helpful, critical readings: Janice Anderson, Carole Blair, Martha Cooper, Gary Copeland, Gerard Hauser, Mary Mander, Gerald Phillips, Lawrence Prelli, Dianne Taylor, and Donna Weimer. I am grateful for their counsel.

Dean Stanley F. Paulson, Associate Dean Thomas F. Magner, and my Department Head, Robert S. Brubaker, all of the College of Liberal Arts at Penn State, assisted me by granting released time and assistance for research during the book's preparation.

My wife, Charolette C. Gregg, typed most of the permutations of the manuscript and prepared the index, as well as providing support throughout all the phases of this project. For other secretarial assistance and much of the typing of the final draft, I thank Joyce Diehl, Linda Harer, and Diane Roan.

I gratefully acknowledge the help of all of these persons and others who put up with the rehearsal of my ideas. They know, as do I, that if there are shortcomings in this work, they remain mine alone.

> Richard B. Gregg
> Linden Hall
> Centre Hall, Pennsylvania
> February 1984

SYMBOLIC INDUCEMENT AND KNOWING

1

RHETORIC, KNOWING, AND THE SYMBOLIC

As human beings, we know, and we know that we know. Throughout our intellectual history, we have been building a vast body of knowledge, and at the same time we have consciously reflected about how it is that we know, and how it is that we ought to know. Across recorded time, answers to questions about knowledge and knowing stand as markers denoting philosophical schools of thought. Such answers have influenced the ways we interacted with our environment and with our fellow human beings, played a part in shaping our institutions, and in fact constrained all of the phenomena of human culture. We often think of these historical developments in a linear fashion, but there is an inevitable circularity to intellectual history. New knowledge must issue from what is already known; our reflections and speculations about our processes of knowing are necessarily limited by what it is that we know at the moment of reflection.

In the introduction to *Human Understanding*, Toulmin provides an example of such circularity in his discussion of the seventeenth century. He points out that while René Descarte and John Locke developed differing theories regarding human knowing, they and their followers accepted three fundamental intellectual tenets of the time. First, operating without an adequate understanding of evolutionary change over historical time, they believed in a fixed order in nature that could be mastered by humans operating with principles of understanding that were universal and fixed. Second, they differentiated between mind and matter, the latter understood to be inert while the former, involving choice and reason, was believed to be the result of nonmaterial phenomena. A consequence of this belief, of course, was the mind-body dichotomy, which led to profound misconceptions that have existed in one form or another down to the present day. The third tenet Decartes, Locke, and others accepted without question was that the epistemic criterion for certainty was to be found in Euclidean geometry which provided the standard against which all knowledge should be measured.[1]

To acknowledge the circularity in our conscious reflection on the nature of our knowledge cannot be taken to mean that we are forever trapped in

3

the same circle. As in the rest of nature, there is an evolutionary trend in our intellectual development, so that our circularity changes over time. In our time, says Toulmin, we can no longer consider the process of human knowing the way seventeenth-century thinkers did, because we know more than they knew. We now know about the principles of natural evolution and realize that matter is in a constant state of flux over time. We know that what was then thought of as mind cannot be localized in one center in the human nervous structure, but that we possess a highly complex, distributed neurological system operating in interaction with the environment. We know that mathematical certainties are confined to mathematical systems, and that one of the attractions of mathematics is that it is a purely human construct. Thus it is that all across the domains of knowledge treating of complex phenomena, from biology to psychology, the constrictions of seventeenth-century thought have been or are being discarded.

Nearly four decades before Toulmin wrote of the need to put aside the conceptual remnants of the seventeenth century, Langer declared them to be withered and dead, and she announced that different questions were being raised and new concepts forged in the dawning of a new philosophical age. The influence of scientific empiricism, she wrote, was fading with the realization of the "surprising truth that *our sense-data* are primarily symbols."[2] The recognition of the power of symbolism was, for Langer, the cue to the inaugural of a new perspective on human understanding. By the "power of symbolism," Langer meant "the use of symbols to attain, as well as to organize, belief":

> Of course, this alters our conception of intelligence at a stroke. Not higher sensitivity, not longer memory or even quicker association sets man so far above other animals that he can regard them as denizens of a lower world: no it is the power of using symbols—the power of *speech* that makes him lord of the earth. So our interest in the mind has shifted more and more from the acquisition of experience, the domain of sense, to the *uses* of sense data, the realm of conception and expression.[3]

The human mind, Langer emphasized, is not the passive recipient of sense data, but it is actively engaged in structuring data for use. It is the *using* of symbols that Langer focused on, symbols in relation to conception, to expression, specifically in relation to speech. As we shall see in the chapters that follow, in our day we need to reshape some aspects of Langer's statement. Nonetheless, the fundamental import of Langer's comments has been substantially bolstered by a great deal of research in the years since she wrote. To comprehend the processes of human understanding, we must make the best sense we can of the symbolic activities that underlie

4

such phenomena as conceptualization and expression. Langer's emphasis on the *uses* of symbols, on the *action* of the mind, indicates that symbolic processing and structuring must be our major concerns.

The task is formidable and demands a synthesis from diverse areas of study because the subject is cross-disciplinary in its nature. Until very recent years, the problem of trying to discern and describe symbolic processing in any holistic way was largely ignored. Bickerton's comments regarding our understanding of conceptualization hold for symbolic processing as well:

> Our understanding is deficient because neurologists have considered the more "metaphysical" implications of their task as somebody else's business, because "continuists" of the grunt-groan-or-gesture school have thought that the nature of reality is self-evident and therefore didn't need to be constructed, and because philosophers, who alone could be expected to perceive the problems inherent in perceiving anything at all, have resolutely refused to tie their ballooning speculations down to the nuts-and-bolts of what we already know about what we have in our heads and what we might be expected to be able to do with it. So the whole area slipped between the cracks of the disciplines. But that area still exists, and is crucial in the explanation of human capacities. . . .4

Recently, scholarly ennui has given way to scholarly activity that holds great promise. The old mind-body dichotomy has been mortally wounded by research in such fields of study as biochemistry, biophysics, bioengineering, and physiology. Various studies in the behavioral sciences have undermined the efficacy of the long-standing logic-emotion distinction. The very nature of reason is reopened for exploration from new directions. Philosophers of science are engaged in debate about what it is that constitutes scientific knowledge. Scholars interested in language, language development, and meaning are turning more and more to the general findings of cognitive psychology, and even to the specific findings of neurophysiology, in the attempt to locate the origins of the symbolic manifestations in which they are interested.

Among those who are converging, albeit in different ways, toward the subject of human understanding are scholars of rhetoric. This should not be surprising, for rhetoric and knowing were perceived in relationship by the Greeks of classical antiquity, who had many an intellectual scuffle concerning the nature of human knowledge and the role of rhetoric, both real and proper, in its formulation. The roots of this general approach to the problem can be found in the fifth and fourth centuries B.C. in Greece, when a coalescing of social and intellectual factors led to remarkable advances in thought. Among the contributing factors were an increased opportunity for leisure and meditation that enhanced social exchange, the invention of coinage and the stimulation of trade, and the political climate encouraged by the unique characteristics of the Greek city state. These factors and others combined to produce new attitudes of criticism toward received knowledge. Central to all of this activity was the invention of the written alphabet which allowed the Greeks to capture ideas and hold them still for personal and public inspection in ways not possible in a strictly oral culture. With the aid of this new technology, inconsistencies among ideas could be seen more clearly, opposites could be examined together, and the implicational relationships of ideas could begin to be constructed. New modes of categorization began to develop, and new methods for the demonstration of "knowledge" were formulated.

This was highly sophisticated symbolic activity goaded by an underlying symbolic lure, the urge to secure certain knowledge where possible by the use of proper demonstrative methods. Encouraged by such a stimulating intellectual context, the Greeks developed systems and modes of argument that came to be distinguished in terms of the degrees of certainty and probability they produced. Despite the great impact of the written alphabet, the Greeks still thought about the processes of knowledge demonstration in terms appropriate to the processes of an oral culture, because orality had provided the primary means of preserving and transmitting the culture for centuries. Thus an interesting kind of paradox occurred; the ability to preserve thought in writing led not only to intellectual advances but to new understandings of the workings of intellect itself, while prominent Greek scholars, including Plato, inveighed against the untrustworthiness of thought preserved in writing.5 Demonstrating knowledge through the methods of oral argument was believed by many to provide the best means of achieving "truth."

Among the modes of oral demonstration developed were systems and methods designated as "rhetoric." There was great dispute concerning the value of rhetoric in the establishment of "knowledge," but over the years in our Western intellectual tradition those Greek scholars who assigned rhetoric a secondary role carried the day. They were drawn more to such formal areas of knowledge as mathematics, where they believed certainty could be reached through methods of dialectic and logic. Seventeenth-century philosophers were not the first to respond to the lure of mathematical demonstration,6 and Plato was the first great philosophical pursuer of the lure.

It is not my purpose to trace the relationship of rhetoric and knowing through history. Suffice it to say that the relationship was tenuous and sometimes strained. At worst, rhetoric was understood to be the purveyor of falsity and sham. In a slightly more optimistic vein it was depicted as a "handmaiden" to truth, necessary for the dissemination of true knowledge to those not intelligent enough to see it on their own. In yet more positive perspectives, rhetoric was thought to constitute certain techniques or strategies for encouraging cooperation and productive decision making. In theoretical perspectives such as these, the establishing of knowledge always preceded the employment of rhetoric. Rhetoric could operate on the basis of what was known but it played no role in discovering or structuring knowledge.

In our own age, however, there are scholars who conceive the relationship to be reversed so that what becomes known is discovered and tested through various modes of rhetorical discourse. For instance, Chaim Perelman asserts that we engage in philosophical tasks of epistemological investigation through argumentation. Therefore, he believes a theory of argument ought to precede a theory of knowledge:

> The role of decision in the working out of our ideas has been far too much neglected in the theory of knowledge. By taking account of the reasons we have for deciding in a particular way, or of the techniques of reasoning by which decisions or the facts are linked to theoretical systems, we hope to be able to reintegrate in a theory of knowledge aiming at being rationalist the whole of the vast field now outside it, a field which includes among other things the very methods by which the theory of knowledge is developed. . . . The reasons on which our decisions are based consist more often than not of opinions which we consider the most probable, probability in this case being in any case rarely susceptible of quantitative determination. These opinions are worked out by means of reasonings which depend neither on self-evidence, nor on analytic logic, but on presumptions whose investigation depends on a theory of argumentation. 7

Perelman and Mme. Olbrechts-Tyteca had already published in French the work later to appear in English as *The New Rhetoric: A Treatise on Argumentation,* 8 an attempt to establish a theory of rhetoric that would function as the basis for a philosophy of knowledge.

Richard McKeon is another philosopher who sees communication as playing an antecedent role in the acquisition of knowledge. McKeon is concerned with the problem of establishing common agreements or working agreements in a technological age amidst a great plurality of interests. For McKeon, in such a context "knowledge is accomplished in situations of discussion, action, and dispute,"9 and "truths emerge in the oppositions of opinions. . . ."10 According to McKeon, "no marks antecedent to discussion suffice to distinguish truth from error."11

> Discourse takes its being and its meaning in a context of deliberation, judgment, and demonstration. When they are universalized as methods

of science, art, and action, discourse is their embodiment. It constitutes or constructs their media of communication and expression; it discovers or creates their subject matter, it sets or expresses their objectives; and it establishes or applies the criteria of their success. The intelligible structure of the universe and the objective structure of thought have been transformed into the consequential structure of discourse. The sequences and consequences of things, thoughts, actions, and statements are inseparable, and they establish connections between fact and theory, fact and value, fact and fiction, fact and nonexistence, which in turn make the connections of sequences in discourse possible and intelligible. 12

Harold Zyskind envisions the role of rhetoric in the structuring of knowledge in a way very similar to McKeon's view. Whenever our interests compel us to interact with the raw data of experience, "rhetorical logic" is involved. Such logic is employed because of the human tendency to search for and structure patterns of action and thought. Rhetorical logic, says Zyskind, is not derivative, but primary, because "there is no a priori set of conditions defining the sorts of relations which constitute a pattern. . . ." Accordingly, the way is open in processes of observation and experience for the discovery "and testing of new modes of relation as bases for probabilistic inference. . . ." 13

The perspectives I have briefly alluded to feature rhetoric as method. In other words, certain *modes* of argumentation, or of articulating problems, testing solutions, or exploring ideas will lead to knowledge. There are other perspectives which place emphasis on the symbolic nature of humans in ways that correspond to Langer's view. For example, Wayne Booth describes the human as "a self-making-and-remaking, symbol-manipulating creature, an exchanger of information, a communicator, a persuader and manipulator, an inquirer." 14 Because we are all symbolic creatures, says Booth, "we are often successful in exchanging ideas, emotions, and purposes, using not only words but a fantastically rich set of other symbolic devices, ranging from facial expressions that seem much more resourceful than those available to other animals, bodily stances, dancing, music, mathematics, painting, sculpture, stories, rituals, and manipulation of social groups in war and politics." 15 From this perspective, says Booth, the supreme purpose of rhetoric would not be to persuade others to preconceived points of view, but "to engage in mutual inquiry or exploration." 16

It would be difficult in our time to locate any scholar of rhetoric who has more thoroughly explored and employed the symbolic perspective than Kenneth Burke. In all of his work Burke assumes that the human is a "symbol-using, symbol-making, and symbol-misusing animal." 17 "But,"

asks Burke, "can we bring ourselves to realize just what the formula implies, just how overwhelmingly much of what we mean by 'reality' has
been built up for us through nothing but our symbol systems?"18

> If we defined man first of all as the tool-using animal . . . our definition
> would not be taking into account the "priority" of its very own nature as
> a definition. Inasmuch as definition is a symbolic act, it must begin by
> explicitly recognizing its formal grounding in the *principle* of definition
> as an act. 19

We have, then, two fundamental perspectives which emerge from these
statements; the first grants authoritativeness to methods of arguing or
demonstrating, of justifying and verifying, and symbolizing would be
constrained by such methods; the second emphasizes the structuring of
knowledge through symbolic processing, and such processing would be
prior to the employment of any particular demonstrative method for it
would be involved in the structuring of the method. Within these positions
of fundamental difference, there are further ambiguities. Perelman would
restrict the kinds of knowing established through argument to matters of
opinion, which, in popular parlance would bring to mind issues primarily
involving philosophy, ethics, political matters, religion, literary taste, aesthetics, and so on. The kinds of knowledge generated by such formal systems as logic and mathematics, and knowledge in areas typically referred
to as the "hard sciences" would be beyond rhetoric's purview. McKeon on
the other hand conceives rhetoric to be an architectonic art which would
constrain the structuring of all fields of knowledge. Zyskind, while interested in rhetoric as method, provides a kind of ambiguous bridge to symbolizing when he talks of the "processes of observation and experience."
Operating from a position of similar ambiguity, Booth refers both to processes of "enquiry and exploration" and to the symbolic processes through
which we create "realities." In the writings of Burke, the symbolic is clearly prior to any set of methods or procedures for discovery.

The ambiguities remain, in one form or another, in the cluster of essays
written over the last decade and a half that continue to explore the rheto-
ric-knowledge interface. In 1968, Robert Scott published an essay with
the bold title, "On Viewing Rhetoric as Epistemic."20 Arguing that human truths are contingent rather than immutable, Scott says, "Insofar as
we can say that there is truth in human affairs, it is in time; it can be the
result of a process of interaction at a given moment. Thus rhetoric may be
viewed not as a matter of giving effectiveness to truth but of creating
truth."21 A decade later, Scott noted that a certain life had begun to grow
around the perspective he introduced, and he amplified some of his earlier
comments by way of reiterating his belief that the perspective could prove

9

fruitful.22 Several years later, following a review of articles (which appeared in 1976 and 1977) in speech communication journals, Michael Leff noted the apparently "emerging consensus" that supported Scott's belief, and that seemed to amount to the assertion of a fundamental break with established rhetorical tradition. Leff summarized the various positions pertinent to the rhetoric-epistemic relationship as he found them in the literature he examined, and he concluded that "the epistemic view, in any of its forms, alters the assumptive ground of modern rhetorical theory, and it thereby reopens some basic questions about the nature of rhetorical theory."23 "The common goal," said Leff, "is to establish the epistemic basis for the study of rhetoric."24

ESTABLISHING A PERSPECTIVE

The first steps taken in recent years are understandable attempts to locate just where in the epistemic realm rhetoric may properly be located. Generally such attempts seem to take one of three forms: (1) the suggestion is made that rhetoric is appropriately related only to certain areas or kinds of knowledge; (2) rhetoric is properly seen as a set of methods or processes by which knowledge is constructed; or (3) rhetoric is associated with a kind of symbolic creativity fundamental to all knowing. There is overlap and ambiguity among these forms, so that one can slip easily from one form to another while contemplating what at first may appear to be form-specific problems. For instance, questions of universal versus relative phenomena are not easily contained within the arbitrary distinctions I have drawn above. We would expect there to be problems with distinctions in the early going.

It is not my purpose to summarize the three directions of early exploration in detail, nor is it my purpose to critique them exhaustively. Such a critique must, I think, await further developments. I want simply to outline the formulations generally, and to raise a question or two regarding each in order to establish the particular perspective I intend to pursue.

Attempts to locate rhetorical phenomena within the larger map of kinds of knowledge have led to establishing arbitrary and questionable boundaries. For instance, some claims are made to the effect that rhetoric is to be located in areas of contingent knowledge. Contingent knowledge, we surmise, must be opposed to certain or immutable knowledge, on the one hand, or it must have to do with degrees of contingency on the other. The argument has been made, for example, that rhetoric is limited to such contingent areas of knowledge as political, social, moral, and religious affairs.25 This claim seems to presume that these areas of contingent knowledge suffer from less certainty than other areas such as the hard sciences. Another argument poses the matter this way: rhetoric is related to a kind of "social knowledge" which more closely corresponds to phenomena of the external world. 26

In light of the post-seventeenth-century intellectual revolution, it is difficult to see how either of these claims can be maintained with rigor. For among the discarded baggage of that philosophical period lie those absolutistic conceptions of knowledge that posited universal, immutable truths, or immutable criteria for the establishment of such truths. The most devastating attacks have come from scholars of the sciences, and their refutation of absolutistic positions has been thorough. In essence, the fundamental claim emanating from contemporary critiques of science is that all knowledge, the scientific variety no less than any other, is theory determined, and as theories change so will what is called "knowledge." Walter Weimer illustrates the matter this way:

> One cannot have a fact without having a prior theory. To see this, consider the following bald instruction: Observe carefully and write down every fact you see. It is clear that the instruction cannot be carried out— for one does not know what, if any, "observation" constitutes a "fact." Observation is a *skill* over and above the passive reception of the raw data of sensory experience. Facts are not picturable, observable entities; instead they are *wholly conceptual* in nature. They do not exist apart from a conceptual scheme. Were there no conceptual scheme available to single out recurrent regularities in it, all that "observation" would disclose would be the chaotic flux of phenomenal experience, the "buzzing confusion" attributed to William James. People with different conceptual schemes live in different worlds; the "facts" of one are not those of the other. 27

At the explicit level, theories are articulated schemas or conceptualizations which pattern or structure meanings. Theories constrain knowing; that is, they direct us to ask certain kinds of questions, suggest the methods and procedures to be used in answering such questions, and throughout, direct us to search for and find certain kinds of data. They are, as Weimer puts it, "generational" and they "sanction inferences to unobserved cases." 28

Theories are open to modification and change; indeed the intellectual history of the human race is the history of theoretical change. As physicist David Bohm states, "the basic action of science is seen to involve *perception of what is new and different* from moment to moment. In this regard it is similar to the relevant activity in everyday life, which is also such a kind of perception." 29 At the explicit or discursive level, then, science provides us with ever evolving and changing conclusions rather than immutable truths. The point with regard to the claims of "absolutes" is, all knowing is contingent. 30

The second distinction noted above turns matters a slightly different way. It holds that rhetoric is involved in the construction of what is called "social knowledge" or "explicit knowledge." Those who hold this position do not deny the possibility of private or implicit meaning and experiencing, but they clearly make the presumption that experiences which either cannot be or are not reproduced in articulate and discursive ways do not constitute knowledge. Those human attitudes and feelings which remain inarticulate and hidden from public exposure are "pre-rhetorical-and-unfounded."[31]

At the heart of this position, is the belief that various processes of verification must be undertaken in order to certify the knowledge status of claims. Valid verification processes must somehow transcend subjective feelings; there must be some phenomena "out there" beyond our own individual skins to tell us we have a right to know what we think we know. As Brummett puts it: "Now the question is this: if objective reality does not exist, where will people get the reality that we do have? Which is to say, where will we get the meaning we have? The answer is that people get meanings from other people through communications."[32] The "intersubjectivist position" can be expressed in one of several ways; it can hold that in certain areas of knowledge testing and validation of ideas can only occur through the processes of communication, or it can hold that all knowledge is social knowledge since "whatever we know is 'known' because there are objective public standards for deciding such things."[33]

But, when we come to deal with matters of "knowing," significant difficulties arise pertinent to this kind of distinction. Human knowing and understanding consist of more than that which can be rendered explicit through any symbol system; in fact, formal symbol systems are capable of reflecting or creating only a portion of what we know. Whatever symbol systems and meaning are, contemporary studies demonstrate that they are not identical; literal symbol sequences sometimes refer to meaning complexes that are far more complicated than the literal explicit representation, and sometimes the meaning patterns referred to are far more simple.[34] Now, it can certainly be argued that the various systems of human symbols interact with, and to an extent constrain, the ways we know. It is a mistake, however, to argue that they exhaustively represent all cognitive activity. They are possible because of human cognitive capacity, and knowledge springs from that entire capacity, not just from explicit systems of symbols.

Ludwig Wittgenstein is one who advanced the argument that the "inner processes" of human cognitive activity depend upon "outer processes." For Wittgenstein, to talk about knowing was to refer to matters that had somehow been verified publicly. His case rested on the notion that language created reality, that language was a social convention requiring the possibility of correction by others, and consequently that public verification and meaning were essential to the formulation of knowledge. He further argued that a private language was impossible. His conclusion, consequently, was that all meaning is social. 35

Under close examination, however, Wittgenstein's position crumbles. Critics have demonstrated that his distinction between public and private memory is untenable, that it is possible to discover rules to determine whether a private language is being used correctly, that languages do refer to personal and private data, and that such data are not only valid, but inevitably involved in an act of communication. They further show that by Wittgenstein's criteria, no language is possible. 36

George Steiner, who is a multilingual student of language translation notes that one of Wittgenstein's mistakes lies in his unwillingness to admit that words can refer simultaneously to private meanings and to social or public meaning. Steiner points out that meaning is full of associative matter composed of personal experience and subconscious phenomena. Such associative contexts vary from individual to individual, and can be seen to run the gamut from autistic babel to public banality:

> Active inside the "public" vocabulary and conventions of grammar are pressures of vital association, of latent or realized content. Much of this content is irreducibly individual and, in the common sense of that term, private. When we speak to others we speak "at the surface" of ourselves. We normally use a shorthand beneath which there lies a wealth of subconscious, deliberately concealed or declared associations so extensive and intricate that they probably equal the sum and the uniqueness of our status as an individual person. 37

But the fact that some of what we know is "invisible" in the socially articulated sense does not mean that it is totally outside our awareness, or that we do not respond to it in ourselves and others when we interact.

To put a slightly different face on the problem, Michael Polanyi and others have introduced us to the "tacit" level of knowing, a kind of out-of-awareness level of activity where reside rules and principles of mental operation that underlie all dimensions of meaning. While we can differentiate the tacit from more explicit components of knowing for purposes of discussion, in actual human cognitive activity the distinction turns into a continuum and knowing is formed by the intermingling. Weimer believes that the problem of tacit knowledge *is* the problem of meaning, and he declares that Polanyi is wrong to assert that none of it can ever be known. Indeed, Piaget in his studies of the development of logical and mathematical

13

understanding in children does clearly unveil some of the functions of tacit activity, 38 and other studies appear to have done so as well. 39 The general point to be drawn from this is that we know more than we can talk or write about.

Before leaving this matter we should note that while some level of critical activity is necessary to the formulation of knowledge, and while social interaction can encourage such activity explicitly, social interaction is not essential to formulation of knowledge. Constant checking of the internal and external environments is inherent in all mental activity.

We must conclude that distinctions drawn in the first general approach to the study of rhetoric and knowing, distinctions that mark off contingent knowledge from certain knowledge or social knowledge from personal knowledge, cannot be maintained. Thus we would be mistaken, this early in our probing, to formulate and adhere to distinctions that foreclose the possibility of examining any of the areas or forms of knowing.

The second general approach to the rhetoric-epistemic question identified earlier is one of conceiving rhetoric to be a set of methods or a system of procedures that leads to establishing and certifying knowledge. In his review, Leff finds four senses in which the relationship of rhetoric to knowing is discussed, and three of them hinge on the notion of rhetoric as method or procedure: (1) discourse is taken to have the persuasive force to alter one's perception of an object by locating it within a fixed set of general criteria; (2) a more autonomous kind of knowledge is established through the systematic relating of persons, problems, interests, and actions; (3) rhetoric operates more flexibly than systems of formal logic to secure initial premises in a meta-logical way. Each of these senses assumes social interaction or intersubjective consensus to be essential, and although the precise methods for interaction are not fully spelled out, it seems clear that the force of rhetoric with regard to the establishing or certifying of knowledge occurs through procedural operations.

McKeon is the contemporary scholar who has developed the most encompassing view of rhetoric as method. McKeon treats rhetoric as one of the communication arts, and taken as a whole, he believes the communication arts can be architectonic. By that he means that they contain the principles of all knowledge and thus can be used to create and certify knowledge in any area whatsoever. In McKeon's system grammar is the art of discovering or recovering meaning in various structures, logic is the art of relating sequences of ideas in discourse, dialectic is the art of synthesizing intelligible wholes from parts, and rhetoric is the art of locating or constructing conceptual starting places for knowledge. Rhetoric, thus, is inventive in the true sense of that term. 40 It is the use of *topoi* or commonplaces to bring thoughts together in new and productive ways. McKeon is a firm apostle for his notion that in this age of diversity, his set of ideologically neutral architectonic communication methods ought to be used to discover and construct the truths of the world.

There is nothing wrong with taking rhetoric to be a set of methods or procedures if one wants to do so, though it is a limiting perspective with regard to knowledge. Like a language system, any set of rules or procedures when followed seriously has the potential to influence the way we talk and think. But, like language, explicit rules and procedures do not account for all meaning or cognitive activity, even at the instant of their use. They are reflective or constitutive of a part of cognition only. All sets of explicit methods or procedures, insofar as they have meaning, are emanations of cognitive activity, as are any commitments agreed upon concerning their use. Consequently, a part of what they mean will be informed by cognitive processes that are personal and implicit. And contrary to McKeon's wishes, they can never be nonideological in the broad sense of the term. McKeon does take us to the threshold of cognitive activity when he talks of rhetoric as a creative process, but his orientation is prescriptive rather than descriptive, and he does not see it as germane to his case to ask how the human mind really functions.

The third general position that links rhetoric to knowing does so by associating rhetoric with processes of symbolic creating that are fundamental to all knowing. In a more general sense, the major claim of this position is that all knowing is rhetorical. The rationale for such a viewpoint is compatible with Langer's statement, cited earlier, concerning the significance of symbols and symbolic processes. Briefly put, language is held to be the instrument through which knowledge is constructed; because language is inherently valuative, all knowing is thus rhetorical. Leff points out that this perspective is only incipient in the literature he surveyed, but he concludes that its further development bears watching. 41

Italian philosopher Ernesto Grassi provides us with a recent and extended discussion of the position. Briefly put, Grassi's idea is that there are two kinds of language expression. The first is essentially rational; it provides the reasons or proof in support of claims. The logical end of this kind of expression, says Grassi, is the demand for mathematical symbols that allow us to draw conclusions from initial premises. Rational expression is essentially deductive in nature and is limited to discovering what is already contained in the assumed premises. The second form of language is "original," "inventive," and "imagistic." This form of expression provides us with insight through the presentation of images that bring out the similarities among phenomena by revealing relationships that we did not

15

see before. It is the language of creation; the relationships created by its imagery constitute its "demonstration." "The primacy of imagistic, directive, revelatory language lies in the fact that this is what makes deductions of any kind possible."42 This is the language of rhetoric, says Grassi, and through it alone are we able to arrive at first principles of knowledge. It is "original" speech. Grassi's perspective sharply alters the view of rhetoric because, as he puts it, "Thus the term 'rhetoric' assumes a fundamentally new significance; 'rhetoric' is not, nor can it be the art, the technique of an exterior persuasion; it is rather the speech which is the basis of rational thought."43 He goes on to assert that the kind of analogical knowledge produced by rhetoric "lies at the base of human cognition."44

While fundamentally different from many other views of rhetoric, Grassi's perspective is not new. He himself traces its lineage back through the Italian humanists to the Greeks who thought about the starting assumptions for demonstration as well as the unfolding implicational structure that comprised the processes of demonstration. Aristotle, Plato, and others believed that *archai,* or first principles, had to be mastered by those who would construct the proofs of demonstration, because to "know" the *archai* was to possess true knowledge. The *archai* were to be "known" to a higher degree than the knowledge produced by demonstration; they were not the end products of rationality but were essentially nonrational or prerational in character, arrived at through the intellection of insight. We tend to remember the Greeks for their contributions to rationality, forgetting that they were equally fascinated by nonrational and irrational phenomena. In fact, it is not much of an overstatement to say they were obsessed by such matters. Their struggle to achieve rationality can also be understood as a struggle to escape from those processes that came to be seen as irrational. 45

The rhetorical theories of Cicero and Quintilian also inform Grassi's thinking, but most important is the work of eighteenth-century philosopher Giambattista Vico. Vico placed imagination rather than reason at the base of human knowledge. For Vico it is not the concept, but image and metaphor, that represent the beginning of thought. 46 Grassi's position, with his emphasis on imagistic, revelatory language, is a modern restatement of Vico's ideas.

Grassi is correct to assert that his conceptualization changes our view of rhetoric. Rhetoric becomes more profoundly and intimately associated with the production of knowledge than most other perspectives are willing to posit. There is some ambiguity in his position, but at this point in our discussion it can be productive ambiguity. Insofar as Grassi's conceptualization is based on the notion that all thought takes place through language, it suffers from the same shortcomings attributed earlier to the intersubjectivist position. Human thought is somewhat constrained by, but not confined within, language systems. Thought precedes language. On the other hand, when Grassi talks of a kind of analogical knowledge produced by rhetoric that lies at the base of cognition, he invites us to find the seeds of rhetoric in cognitive activity.

SYMBOLIZING, KNOWING, AND RHETORICAL ACTION

Our brief survey of the current interface between "rhetoric" and "knowing" reveals that a clearly efficacious position has not been worked out. We must also be frank to admit that considerable ambiguity surrounds both of these concepts. That very fact, of course, is part of the problem of trying to delineate the relationship. It might seem that what we need to do is forge clear and sharp definitions of rhetoric and of knowing or knowledge, and then we would better understand the relationship of the two. But our survey indicates there may be a better approach.

I noted earlier that years ago Langer wrote that a new era for understanding human comprehension was begun with a new appreciation of the human potential for symbolization. As a result, our attention turns to "conceptualization" and "expression" as human intellectual activities that are fundamentally important to our comprehension of human behavior generally. But there is something more basic and common to both conceptualizing and expressing; that is human symbolic capacity. Just as birds will fly because they have the capacity to do so, humans will symbolize because such activity is an inherent part of human potential. As Langer pointed out, the need to symbolize is a primary human activity that occurs just because we are innately wired to engage in symbolic behavior. She emphasized that symbolization is "pre-rationative"; "It is the starting point of all intellection in the human sense, and is more general than thinking, fancying or taking action."47 Symbolic activity is fundamental to all that we know to be human.

To be a bit more precise, at the most fundamental level symbolization refers to all that the human mind and brain does. The brain is constantly involved in the structuring of data from the external environment and from within its own activity. In other words, all mind-brain activity is symbolic. Put another way, all human experiencing is the result of brain processing which creates the structures we call "meaning." There is no meaning but that which results from neurophysiological activity. This is not to say that our meanings are inherently and inevitably determined by our neurophysiological activity operating in a vacuum; we have the ability

17

to change our minds, to alter our opinions, to see things in new ways, to reject well-established modes of experiencing. The neurological correlate for this is that the normal human brain literally has the capacity to modify its operations, to correct errant activity, to initiate new processes—and in a literal sense, to rewire portions of itself when conditions seem to warrant. If there are limits to our brains' activity (and it seems reasonable that there are), we are unlikely ever to know them all and equally unlikely ever to reach them.

Despite the fact that there is much we do not know about brain functioning and cognitive processing, there is much that we do know. From studies in neurophysiology, in cognitive psychology, and many cognate areas which examine outward manifestations of neurophysiological and cognitive processes, we know that such processes are not random but are principled. This is to say they are constrained in operation by certain laws or rules or norms. We may refer to these laws, rules, and norms as principles of operation and go on to ask about the relationship between the fundamental principles that operate at the level of neurophysiological-cognitive processing and those principles that underlie such outward behavioral manifestations as individual, group, and public actions. Symbolization can be used to serve a multitude of functions from providing modes of self-expression to constituting "tools" to be used for instrumental purposes to constructing the social phenomena of collective identity. The artifacts we refer to as "our culture," the behaviors and relationships we refer to as "social behaviors," the attitudes and values we think of as forming our "selves," and the symbol systems we use to express ourselves, all partake of the formative principles of symbolizing. It would seem logical, then, to commence an exploration of the relationship of rhetoric to knowing with an examination of these formative principles.

In the following chapters, I propose to examine the relationship of symbolizing, knowing, and rhetorical activity in an inductive fashion. I shall first explore the fundamental nature of symbolic processing. The principles of symbolizing originate in the workings of mind, which function in accordance with the workings of the brain. These coordinate operations are so intertwined and conjoined that I shall be referring to them as the operations of mind-brain. While this hyphenated expression may not seem as felicitous as one would like, it appears to be the only one that can be used to emphasize that the research findings of neurophysiology require us to avoid the misunderstandings that arise from conceptualizing a mind/body dichotomy. My concern will be to describe those principles of cognitive activity that function to produce perception, conceptualization, and expression.

The cognitive principles involved in perception, conceptualization, and expression are the very principles involved in the processes that produce "knowledge." I shall not attempt to define "knowledge," for there are many different kinds of knowledge. There is tacit knowledge, implicit knowledge, discursive knowledge, individual knowledge, commonly held knowledge, emotional knowledge, intellectual knowledge, not to mention scientific knowledge, social scientific knowledge, and humanistic knowledge. "Knowledge," the product of the processes of knowing, is always relative to a particular context. Many times the processes of knowing are also context bound. But the cognitive principles that operate to produce knowledge, while interactive with context, are themselves context invariant. They are operative whenever and wherever human experiencing occurs. With attention focused on cognitive or symbolic principles, our question becomes: How do they function in the total experience of knowing? And my question regarding rhetoric's relation to all this is similarly phrased: How, if at all, does rhetoric function in the total experience of knowing?

In keeping with the inductive spirit of my inquiry, I shall not posit a definition of rhetoric at the outset; rather, I will see whether a concept of rhetoric emerges from the exploration that follows. I do, however, need a starting point, a focus that will help search out those aspects of symbolic experiencing that might properly be called, "rhetorical." To help with this matter, I turn to a statement regarding language and rhetoric that Burke makes in his *Rhetoric of Motives*. He says that rhetoric "is rooted in an essential function of language itself, a function that is wholly realistic, and is continually born anew: the use of language as a symbolic means of inducing cooperation in beings that by nature respond to symbols."48

I take Burke to mean that among the inherent functions of language is that of symbolic inducement. Since a language is a symbol system made possible by the more general symbolic capacity humans possess, and since symbolic inducement is a symbolic function, then it seems reasonable that principles of symbolic inducement can be found among the principles of cognitive activity. Generally speaking, *symbolic inducement refers to those symbolic principles and functions which lead or invite us on to action and which begin in the workings of the mind-brain.* In his lucid explication of the philosophy of Bergson, I. W. Alexander explains a portion of Bergson's thought as follows:

> The preliminary condition of the world so to become "for me" is the development of centres of indetermination at the level of bodily experience itself. As the nervous system becomes more complicated, it develops an ever greater number of possible reactions and motor paths. The brain in

19

particular evolves a highly complex motor apparatus which introduces into its operations degrees of indetermination; it contains an invitation to act, with at the same time leave to wait and even do nothing. 49

I shall be looking for principles of symbolic inducement among the fundamental principles of cognitive processing.

If the fundamental principles of mind-brain operate to structure all of human behavior, then they will function to constrain the structuring and use of any and all human symbol systems. Consequently, it will behoove me to examine a typical symbol system, to get a sense for the way in which mind-brain principles may manifest themselves, for the way in which they may undergo modification and transformation if, in fact, they do, and to determine the interaction of the principles and the symbol system. Here again, I will be specifically interested in principles of symbolic inducement. The particular system I shall examine is language, because it is a system typically and universally employed by humans. There are, of course, other symbolic modes of human expression and communication, but insofar as principles of inducement can be seen to work in and through language we can conclude they are operative in other symbol systems as well.

Finally I must examine these principles in the realm of social and cultural interaction. Among the ways humans can be characterized, it is necessary to acknowledge that we are social beings. We can begin to develop and employ symbol systems in isolation because we innately possess symbolic capacity and because we are inclined to such development and employment. But encouragement toward sophisticated accomplishment occurs most conveniently in social interaction. There are speculative theories, supported by archeological evidence and by the very pervasiveness of social behaviors themselves, which argue that social interaction played an essential role in the survival and evolution of our species. Whether essential or not, we have been social creatures for a very long time, developing the relationships, rituals, groupings, and institutions that form the backbone of cultures. Though we may, at the level of social and cultural interaction, seem several times removed from the fundamental principles of mind-brain, I shall be alive to the possibility that whatever meanings there are at the cultural level must somehow be reflective of those fundamental principles because human meaning begins and ends in the mind-brain. As Mary Midgely says, we are naturally culture-building animals, but "what we build into our cultures has to satisfy our natural pattern of motives." 50

My exploration of the principles of symbolic inducement will occur, then, on three levels. First is the level of mind-brain, where all symbolic activity originates and is completed. Next, there is the level of symbol-system activity, the inevitable consequence of human symbolic capacity. To say that symbol systems, such as languages, or mathematics, or music are inevitable outcomes of the ability to symbolize is not to imply any inevitability regarding the particular forms those outcomes might take. Rather, the statement is simply acknowledgment of the fact that a variety of symbolic systems will be developed by humans in response to a multitude of pressures, purposes, demands, and desires, because such development constitutes natural human generative and responsive behavior. Finally, there is the level of social-cultural interaction, where symbol systems are discursively employed, similarly, in natural human behaviors. While I will separate these levels for purposes of discussion and clarity, in reality they are always mutually interactive in complementary and supportive ways.

THE COMPLEXITY OF SYMBOLIC BEHAVIOR

In the exploration that follows it will be necessary for me to avoid notions of causality, determination, and reductionism that are simplistic. Such modes of conceptualizing betray an apparent need to avoid uncertainty and ambiguity, to seek the satisfactions of closure and the reassurances of completion. They are symptomatic of our tendency to overrationalize human behavior in order to achieve some kind of conceptual control. But they are gross oversimplifications and rarely account, in any strict way, for what is taking place. In their simple and straightforward sense, they have no place in my exploration of symbolizing.

The growth, evolution, and functioning of human symbolic behavior follows the course of human evolution generally. Primate evolution occurs through interaction patterns which paleoanthropologists call closed feedback loops. A closed feedback loop is far from simple; it is multipoled and circular. All of its tendencies are cross-connected, dependent upon each other, act upon each other, and mutually reinforce each other. There is no initiating trigger that causes a closed feedback loop to develop. Rather, it slowly develops through multiple adaptation to various external and internal pressures. To understand the workings of closed feedback loops correctly, one must replace notions of cause with a concept of reciprocal reinforcement. It seems sensible, in light of their mutually reinforcing tendencies, to consider closed feedback loops to be essentially conservative and self-preserving. But it is wrong to consider the human to be forever deterministically bound by them after they have developed. Movement can occur from one feedback loop into another in a kind of quantum leap that has been likened to an apparent *non sequitur*. 51 I think it reasonable

21

to presuppose that human symbolic behavior is closed feedback-loop behavior. Symbolic capacity is innately present in the mind-brain. The manifest processes developing from that capacity are principled, and these underlying principles interact with symbolic manifestations and mutually reinforce each other. Symbolic behaviors act upon and interact with environmental factors and the symbolic behaviors emanating from other humans. There is no simple cause and effect relationship here; rather, we have complex systems of mutual interaction with the potential to guide and constrain all elements of the interaction.

We must begin with what we know about the mind-brain, for whatever symbolizing, knowing, and inducing are, they are functions of mindbody. It is unlikely that we shall ever be able to formulate an existential or metaphysical reality that would provide a definitive explanation or paradigmatic illustration of what symbolic inducement is, because we experience such principles only in their manifestations, in the operation of the human mind-brain and in their outcomes. But we can hope to gain insight into the ways these principles function within the larger contexts of cognition and the more specific contexts of rhetorical behavior.

NOTES

1. Stephen Toulmin, *Human Understanding* (Princeton: Princeton University Press, Paperback Edition, 1977), 13–25.

2. Susanne K. Langer, *Philosophy in a New Key* (New York: Mentor Books, 1958, Ninth Printing), 29. Italics in original.

3. Ibid., 33. Italics in original.

4. Derek Bickerton, *Roots of Language* (Ann Arbor: Karoma Publishers, 1981), 223.

5. For this particular perspective on the Greek experience I am indebted to Tony M. Lentz, "The Oral Tradition of Interpretation: Reading in Hellenic Greece as Described by Ancient Authors," unpublished Ph.D. dissertation (University of Michigan, 1979). See also his "Writing As Sophistry: From Preservation to Persuasion," *Quarterly Journal Of Speech,* 68 (1982), 60–68.

6. G. E. R. Lloyd, *Magic, Reason and Experience* (Cambridge: Cambridge University Press, 1979), and *Polarity and Analogy* (Cambridge: Cambridge University Press, 1966).

7. Chaim Perelman, *The Idea of Justice and the Problem of Argument* (London: Routledge and Kegan Paul, 1963), 97.

8. Chaim Perelman and L. Olbrechts-Tyteca, *The New Rhetoric: A Treatise on Argumentation,* trans. John Wilkinson and Purcell Weaver (Notre Dame: University of Notre Dame Press, 1969).

9. Richard McKeon, "Power and the Language of Power," *Ethics,* 68, No. 2 (January 1958), 112.

10. _____. "Communication, Truth and Society," *Ethics,* 67, No. 2 (January 1957), 99.

11. Ibid.

12. _____. "Discourse, Demonstration, Verification, Justification," *Logique et Analyse,* 11 (1968), 45.

13. Harold Zyskind, "Some Philosophic Strands in Popular Rhetoric," in *Perspectives in Education, Religion and the Arts,* ed. Howard E. Kiefer and Milton K. Munitz (Albany: State University of New York Press, 1970), 387–88.

14. Wayne C. Booth, *Modern Dogma and the Rhetoric of Assent* (Notre Dame: University of Notre Dame Press), 136.

15. Ibid., 113.

16. Ibid., 137.

17. Kenneth Burke, *Language as Symbolic Action* (Berkeley: University of California Press, 1968), 6.

18. Ibid., 5.

19. Ibid., 14.

20. Robert L. Scott, "On Viewing Rhetoric as Epistemic," *CSSJ,* 18 (February 1967), 9–16.

21. Ibid., 13.

22. Robert L. Scott, "On Viewing Rhetoric as Epistemic: Ten Years Later," *CSSJ,* 27 (Winter 1976), 258–66.

23. Michael Leff, "In Search of Ariadne's Thread: A Review of the Recent Literature on Rhetorical Theory," *CSSJ,* 29 (Summer 1978), 84.

24. Ibid., 89–91.

25. Richard Cherwitz, "Rhetoric as 'A Way of Knowing': An Attenuation of the Epistemological Claims of the 'New Rhetoric'," *CSSJ,* 42 (Spring 1977), 207–19.

26. Thomas B. Farrell, "Knowledge, Consensus and Rhetorical Theory," *QJS,* 62 (February 1976), 6–7. See also "Social Knowledge II," *QSJ,* 64 (October 1978), 330–31.

27. Walter Weimer, *Notes on the Methodology of Scientific Research* (Hillsdales, N.J.: Lawrence Erlbaum Associates, 1979).

28. Walter Weimer, "Science as a Rhetorical Transaction: Toward a Nonjustificational Concept of Rhetoric," *Philosophy and Rhetoric,* 10 (Winter 1977), 7.

29. David Bohm, "Science as Perception-Communication," in F. Suppe, ed., *The Structure of Scientific Theories* (Urbana: University of Illinois Press, 1974), 388. Italics in original.

30. For a discussion of two somewhat different perspectives which share the view that scientific knowledge is contingent, see Thomas S. Kuhn, *The Structure of Scientific Revolutions* (Chicago: University of Chicago Press, 1970) and Toulmin, *Human Understanding.*

31. Cherwitz, 210.

32. Barry Brummett, "Some Implications of 'Process' or 'Intersubjectivity': Postmodern Rhetoric," *Philosophy and Rhetoric,* 9 (Winter 1976), 29.

33. Walter M. Carleton, "What Is Rhetorical Knowledge: A Response to Farrell—and More," *QJS,* 64 (October 1978), 325.

34. John Bransford and Jeffery Franks, "The Abstraction of Linguistic Ideas," in *Cognitive Psychology,* 4, 2 (1970), 331–50.

35. L. Wittgenstein, *Philosophical Investigations* (Oxford: Basil Blackwell, 1953), sections 203–315.

23

36. See George Steiner, *After Babel* (London: Oxford University Press, 1975), 161–75.

37. Ibid., 172–73.

38. See Jean Piaget, *Six Psychological Studies* (New York: Random House, 1967), translated by David Elkind; *The Origins of Intelligence in Children* (New York: Basic Books, 1954), and *The Child's Conception of Space* (London: Routledge and Kegan Paul, 1956).

39. See Michael T. Turvey, "Constructive Theory, Perceptual Systems and Tacit Knowledge," in Walter B. Weimer and David S. Palermo, eds., *Cognition and the Symbolic Processes* (Hillsdale, N.J.: Lawrence Erlbaum Associates, 1974), 165–79.

40. Richard McKeon, "Philosophy of Communications and the Arts," in Howard E. Kiefer and Milton K. Munitz, eds., *Perspectives in Education, Religion and the Arts* (Albany: SUNY Press, 1970), 329–50; "Discourse, Demonstration, Verification, Justification," *Logique et Analyse,* 11 (1968), 37–94; "The Uses of Rhetoric in a Technological Age: Architectonic Productive Arts" in Lloyd F. Bitzer and Edwin Black, eds., *The Prospect of Rhetoric* (Englewood Cliffs, N.J.: Prentice-Hall, 1971), 44–63. One of the clearest explanations of McKeon's views of communication as an architectonic art is Gerard A. Hauser and Donald P. Cushman, "McKeon's Philosophy of Communication: The Architectonic and Interdisciplinary Arts," *Philosophy and Rhetoric,* 6 (Fall 1973), 211–34.

41. Leff, 82–84.

42. Ernesto Grassi, "Can Rhetoric Provide a New Basis for Philosophizing? The Humanist Tradition," *Philosophy and Rhetoric,* 11 (Spring 1978), 81.

43. Ernesto Grassi, *Rhetoric as Philosophy: The Humanist Tradition* (University Park: The Pennsylvania State University Press, 1980), 25.

44. Ernesto Grassi, *Rhetoric as Philosophy,* 98. See also his "Rhetoric and Philosophy," *Philosophy and Rhetoric,* 9 (Fall 1976), 200–16.

45. E. R. Dodds, *The Greeks and the Irrational* (Berkeley: University of California Press, 1951).

46. For a discussion of Vico's views on rhetoric, see Alessandro Giuliani, "Vico's Rhetorical Philosophy and the New Rhetoric" in *Giambattista Vico: New Science of Humanity,* eds. G. Tagliacozzo and D. P. Verene (Baltimore: Johns Hopkins University Press, 1976), 31–46.

47. Susanne Langer, *Philosophy in a New Key* (New York: New American Library, 1958), 46–47.

48. Kenneth Burke, *A Grammar of Motives and a Rhetoric of Motives* (Cleveland: World Publishing Company, 1962), 567.

49. I. W. Alexander, *Bergson: Philosopher of Reflection* (New York: Hilary House, 1957), 33.

50. Mary Midgley, *Beast and Man* (New York: New American Library, 1978), 29.

51. Donald Johanson and Maitland Edey, *Lucy: The Beginnings of Humankind* (New York: Simon and Schuster, 1981), 330. For an extended example of a closed feedback loop, see 309–40.

2

PERCEPTION, KNOWING, AND SYMBOLIC INDUCEMENT: THE BEGINNINGS

The most significant evolutionary development for hominids occurred a half-million years or so ago, when our brain size increased by roughly 1,400 cubic centimeters. The average weight of the brain of Australopithicus, our ancestor, was approximately a pound and a half, whereas our average brain today weighs about three pounds. Several concurrent evolutionary developments were directly related to the ability to structure and use language systems. The human chewing apparatus and associated facial architecture diminished in size. Our ancestors' teeth, for example, were larger than ours, though no more efficient in crushing power. One of the inferences drawn from the discovery of this change is that the hominid was beginning to make meat a more prominent dietary item, and the mixed diet of meats and plants improved our ancestors' ability to survive. The desire for meat necessitated hunting activities which in turn influenced the social-communal lives of our forebears.1 It is also probable that facial changes influenced the hominids' capacity to produce vocal sounds.2

Archeological evidence also indicates that hominids developed additional flexibility and skill in hand maneuverability. It surely is no coincidence that there is evidence of accompanying technological innovations; for example, bone and wood tools and weapons date to this period. Not surprisingly, during the same time a certain aesthetic sense revealed itself: stone and bone figurines, rock sculptures, wall paintings, and bone and rock artifacts in burial arrangements. Such achievements can be directly related to the nature of the brain expansion that occurred concomitantly. Neurophysiological scholarship has determined that, in addition to the neural changes that created the possibility for the achievements just mentioned, there were enlargements in the temporal lobe where the capacity for visual memory, sensory integration, and speech reside, and in the frontal lobes which seem related to the human's ability to initiate a task and concentrate upon it until it is completed. A further relevant phenomenon was the development of certain convolutions of the brain resulting from the brain's enlargement. These portions of the brain are uncommitted to either sensory or motor functions at birth but seem programmed to undertake certain functions described by Wilder Penfield as "the transactions of the mind."3 We can never know exactly the causal relationships among all of these developments, but it seems appropriate to suggest that they occurred in an interactive way and in response to factors internal to the organism as well as to pressure and opportunities existing in the environment. There is no ground for presupposing exclusively external developmental forces. In any case, we can be certain that our present capacity for symbolic activity of whatever form springs from the changes in brain structure we have been noting.

Discussion of the complete anatomy of the brain is not germane to our present purpose. The activities of the brain that are of immediate interest are those that occur in the higher cortical areas devoted to cognition. These are activities of what we might call the mid-brain, whose transactions have to do with "feeling" states and certain processes involved with interpretation of specific kinds of data. Here and throughout the brain, various sorts of transmission networks are at work—there are five kinds of electrical transmission in operation, chemical signals governed by at least five families of chemical regulators are generated, and the recent discovery of assorted peptides promises new revelations concerning emotional states. All these various signal or messenger systems, conducted via the neuronal structure of the brain, provide the internal materials which fashion what we refer to as "perception," "knowledge," "feeling," "judgment," or, in other words, our meaning and experience. 4

Some knowledge of fundamental neurophysiological activity is useful in understanding symbolic behavior in general and symbolic inducement in particular. Accordingly, I shall attempt to describe, in general terms, the operations of the messenger systems within the brain, drawing from the description such principles of operation as seem to be of inescapable importance. To test whether one can reasonably infer a strong correlation between these principles and such phenomena as perception, thought, talk, and other overt behavior, we shall examine closely the neurophysiological principles involved in vision, tracing them in their transformations through perception to behavior. The visual system offers heuristic promise for understanding symbolic processes because it is dominant among the human sensory systems and because it is the sensory system that has been most closely studied. If neurophysiological principles can be shown to guide visual experience, we shall have reason to believe that at the most fundamental level of human neurological activity we can locate the foundational network of inducement for all of symbolic behavior. In other words we shall have identified some of the principles that lead to action and that endure through mental transformations to shape symbolic actions in general, including what are referred to as rhetoric and knowledge.

THE INTERACTION OF BRAIN AND EXPERIENCE

Any discussion of human behavior must square with what is known about the neurophysiology of the brain. To take any other position would be to continue the archaic mind-body dichotomy. Evidence abounds to illustrate the interlocking interactions of what have been traditionally referred to as brain and mind.

There are studies of brain-impaired victims whose behavior and thought processes are rendered aberrant by their neurophysiological condition. Parietal lesions, for example, can lead patients to feel that their limbs are moving when, in fact, they are absolutely still. Or a patient may strike a match to light a cigarette but, instead of completing the lighting movement, simply hold the match until it burns the fingers. A hemiplegic may shave only one side of his face, comb only one half of his or her hair, or dry only one side of the body after a shower. When asked to draw a clock face, hemiplegics typically put figures on only one side of the dial. They cannot, of course, tell time. Various studies have also shown that when the delicate mechanisms of chemical balance in the brain are upset by injection of certain kinds of drugs, hallucinatory states can occur. Hallucinations can also be induced by shortages of vitamin B_6 in a diet. In all cases like these the close interdependence of neurophysiological structures and states of experiencing is direct and clear.

It is equally clear that what has been referred to as "mind" can affect neurophysiological functioning. Body metabolism can be changed by verbal suggestion, for example. The suggestion is not made directly; one cannot induce the secretion of enzymes by ordering them secreted. But if one imagines that one has just eaten a fatty meal, the enzyme, lipase, which digests fat is secreted and will show up in the urine. If one imagines that a high-protein meal has been consumed, pepsin and trypsin are secreted. Subjects have been taught to control their heartbeats and blood pressures through cognitive effort alone. Recognition of this interaction between cognition and neurophysiological functions and states has led scholars of neurophysiology and cognitive activity to use such phrases as "the purposeful brain" or "the mindful brain."

The organization and functioning of the brain turn out to be more complex and sophisticated with each new neurological discovery. Scientists are just beginning to understand some of the features of the chemical systems of the brain, and there is reason to believe that they will learn a great deal more than is now known about emotion and feeling as the chemical frontier is further explored. Because this body of knowledge is incomplete, our search for the principles of symbolic inducement will be necessarily incomplete. It can, however, be significantly suggestive.

We are unlikely ever to know all there is to know about the function of the mind-brain. Friedrich Hayek argues persuasively that "any apparatus of classification must possess a structure of a higher degree of complexity than is possessed by the objects which it classifies; and that, therefore, the capacity of any explaining agent must be limited to objects with a structure possessing a degree of complexity lower than its own."[5]

The most sophisticated instrument we have for understanding the mind is the mind itself, and thus, as Hayek's argument goes, we will never possess an analytical instrument powerful enough to understand completely the workings of the mind. We are unlikely ever to understand all of its operations in specific terms, and we will never be able to predict its operations because we will not have all the knowledge necessary to do so. And even if we approached such wisdom we could be foiled because the mind has the capacity to alter its rules of operation at any time, or, for that matter, to make up new rules. It does not follow, however, that we are destined to understand nothing of the mind's functions.

We can hope to understand how the mind works in principle. This applies to the functioning of the mind-brain and also to the functioning of symbolic inducement. We shall never understand the systems of inducement in their entirety, since the possibilities of their manifestation lie embedded in the total cognitive complexity of the mind. Fortunately, however, it is not essential here to achieve the level of comprehension required of a neurophysiologist. We do not have to worry over how many milliseconds one type of synapse will remain open when activated, as compared to some second type of synapse. It will be enough to know that time differentials do exist, and that they can co-exist. This much knowledge supports the general condition of the brain's complexity. At some future time it may be discovered that a more complete accounting for symbolic behavior must include precise information regarding, e.g., synapse activity, but if that is so, that fact will further demonstrate the condition of complexity.

What is the nature of such complexity? It can be illustrated by considering the inadequacy of our language for describing mind-brain functioning. Language lends itself to expression of mind-body distinctions, to portrayal of static processes and mechanistic procedures. But the brain, continually active and functioning holistically, exhibits none of these characteristics. Models of switchboard mechanisms or computers of whatever degree of complexity are hopelessly inept representations of mind-brain functions. Furthermore, written language is a communicative technology that specially represents active processes as more or less static entities. That kind of symbol system offers clear advantages in certain circumstances. When we can hold something still, we can move about it at any pace we choose, examining parts, noting their relationships, memorizing their labels. But if we are examining phenomena whose essence is realized only in complicated, ongoing, and everchanging movement, the linearly static nature of written language becomes inadequate to the demands of the explanatory task. So it will be with any written description of the mind-brain process. The mind-brain is ever active because the patterns of neuronal firing that constitute a part of its nature never cease, though they may vary in tempo. It is helpful to understand a pattern that can be described as movement from receptor neurons through the net of intermediary neurons to the motor neurons, but we lose the picture if we do not remember that there are simultaneous patterns moving from motor neurons through the intermediary net to receptor neurons, and that at the same time there can be horizontal, patterned firing all through the intermediary network. All of these patterns have the capacity to modify themselves, and wholly new patterns may form at any time. We must always remember that the principles of these patterned activities exist in a context of constant activity, even though available ways of speaking or writing about them obscure this fact.

The brain is an elaborate network of cell structures, the fundamental unit of which is the neuron. The typical estimate of the number of neurons that the central nervous system comprises is on the order of a hundred billion, give or take a factor of ten. Evidence indicates that no two neurons are the same, though they function similarly in terms of principle. A neuron is composed of a cell body, a network of fine threads called dendrites that connect with nearby cells, and one major fiber, called the axon, which may be several feet in length. Generally speaking, the dendrites and cell body pick up incoming signals that are integrated and balanced in the cell body, and the cell body may then transmit signals through the axon to terminals from which they are distributed to a new set of neurons. Neurons emit their messages when a certain stimulus threshold is surpassed, and the act of firing lowers the threshold so that the neuron will fire more readily on the next similar occasion, thus reinforcing its own future activity. This seemingly simple action is complicated, however, because the arrival of stimuli may reset the threshold without the occurrence of firing, and chemical changes in the brain may reset whole sets of neuronal thresholds. One neuron may receive inputs from hundreds or thousands of other neurons; some of the inputs encourage neuronal firing while others simultaneously act as inhibitors. The cell body of the neuron goes through a checking activity in which it weighs the "ayes" against the "nays" and then acts accordingly; thus the balancing activity referred to above. 6 The contact point where information is transmitted from one neuronal structure to another is termed a synapse, and a typical neuron may have as many as 10,000 synapses.

The multitude of cell structures within the brain comprise three more holistic networks which can be referred to as the sensory, the motor, and the associative networks. By far the largest number of neuronal structures fall within the associative category so a great deal of the activity of the mind must occur here. All of these neurons are located in what is called the "grey matter" of the brain which is a few millimeters thick. The bulk of space, referred to as "white matter," consists of an extremely complicated network of cross connections among all parts of the brain. The secret of human intelligence and of symbolic activity seems to lie in the interconnectivity of the brain, not in the size of the brain, though the expansion in size made certain symbolic processes possible.7 Now we must see what the implications of this neurophysical interconnectivity are for symbolic activity.

THE PRINCIPLES OF STRUCTURING AND MONITORING

The brain is not inert or passive, waiting for the sensory apparatus to come in contact with external stimulation in order to initiate brain activity. The brain is active, is operative prior to birth, and initiates activity by ordering the sensory network to respond to certain structures of information. The neuronal structures of the sensory systems are never activated individually, but always in relation to and coinciding with other neuronal structures. Thus patterns of neurons become activated. Although the neuronal patterns are not isomorphic with phenomena in the external environment, they correspond in that it is pattern or structure in the environment that is "sensed."

One feature of pattern firing, rhythm, is interesting to think about because of its ubiquitous presence, not only in the brain, but throughout the processes and activities of the body. The unstimulated brain is characterized by uniform cortical activity with all cortical cells firing in unison. When the brain concentrates on stimuli, the pattern of regularity gives way to more complex and uneven firing patterns as groups of cells undertake their own particular functions. In conditions of deep meditation, the dozen-or-so-per-second alpha rhythms are replaced by much slower four-to-six-per-second theta rhythms. These rhythmic patterns are obviously important to overall brain activity, but their specific roles remain unclear. A little is known, however. Local abnormalities of rhythm can be an indication of a blood clot, and more universal abnormalities of rhythm can be the harbingers of epileptic attacks. We know, also, that messages are received and transmitted rhythmically across the brain.

It is important to recognize that the patterned activation of sensory neuronal systems is an act of classification. That is, the information in the external environment which is attended to by the human nervous system is "noticed" in light of certain characteristics that the neuronal structure

30

groups together, establishing relationships among segments of information. It is not accurate to say the sensory networks respond to patterns; it is more appropriate to say that the patterned firing of the brain constructs patterns from information provided by the environment. Because the patterned firing occurs in response to orders from motor neurons in the brain, an act of abstraction always precedes an act of specification.

Ernst Cassirer, whose three volume work on *The Philosophy of Symbolic Forms* was completed in the first half of this century, still provides one of the most satisfactory, non-technical explanations of the phenomena of mental structuring:

> In place of the vague demand for a similarity of content between image and things, we now find expressed a highly complex logical relation, a general intellectual *condition,* which the basic concepts of physical knowledge must satisfy. Its value lies not in the reflection of a given existence, but in what it accomplishes as an instrument of knowledge, in a unity of phenomena, which the phenomena must produce out of themselves. A system of physical concepts must reflect the relations between objective things as well as the nature of their mutual dependency, but this is only possible insofar as these concepts pertain from the very outset to a definite, homogeneous intellectual orientation. 8

This process of structural classification is followed, in principle, at all levels of brain activity as incoming messages work their ways from the sensory through the associational to the motor levels of the brain. But the process of message transmission is neither simple nor linear as we shall now see.

Hayek provides a hypothetical, explanatory example of the classificatory activity of message transformation systems. 9 Sensory perception can be understood as an act of complex, simultaneous, multiple grouping. Suppose that we have a number of balls to be sorted. No two are the same size, and no two have anything in common that is not also held in common with every other ball. Such a set of conditions would result in a situation where the criteria for classification would not be found objectively in the balls themselves but would have to be located in the processes that constitute the act of classifying. Thus, through an act of classification, balls the size of 16, 18, 28, and 40 millimeters might be grouped together in category A, while balls with diameters of 17, 22, 30, and 35 millimeters might be grouped together in category B, and so on. At the same time, the process of classification could occur in yet other ways so that the phenomena being dealt with would receive multiple classification. Thus, we might suppose that as the balls are placed in receptacles they also trigger certain light displays, some triggering red displays and others green displays, with no correlation between the particular display lighted and the particular receptacles into which they are placed. The same ball could at once belong to two different groupings of classifications. One can conceive of yet other ways in which the balls might be grouped together, so the process of classification would be multiple rather than singular. It may often be that various groups of receptor neurons are alert to similar stimuli. Further, certain sets of stimuli often occur in concert with other sets of stimuli. Finally, certain sets of stimuli will regularly occur when the organism is in a given state of balance. As a result of such conditions and forces, the impulses that constitute neural actions with regard to individual complexes of stimuli may themselves evoke other complexes of impulse. Hayek calls such complexes "following impulses." We see, then, that classification, as a principle, is at the heart of acts of sensory perception, that the outcomes of the principle are simultaneously multiple in manifestation, and that the principle is activated by internal conditions and in relation to external environments.

The principle of classification continues to function throughout the neural structure as messages travel on their ways to motor centers in the brain. The categories established in the primary act of perception become the bases for further classification, and this abstractional process continues through the points of synapse which join one neural structure to another until the end point is reached. At this level, the act of classifying is one that operates with the classifications of sets of stimuli and sets of responses that occurred prior to the final act. In addition to classification, two other enduring principles of neural behavior can be observed. First, the act of classifying is also an act of abstraction. In addition, the interrelationships of the acts of perceptual classification are hierarchical in nature as movement toward the motor centers results in higher and higher levels of abstraction. The possible combinations of neuronal networks are so many and so sophisticated that the human mind is incapable of understanding all of them. Something more powerful than the human mind would be needed to reach this level of understanding and, of course, no such instrument is available. Indeed, since the central nervous system has the power constantly to modify and re-wire itself in light of internal or external factors, it seems not irresponsible to regard the possible combinations as infinite.

We must understand, however, that the classifying activities of the brain-mind do not form a single hierarchical structure with one locus of control; rather, they constitute groupings of hierarchies, each with its own control point. In the human neurological system there is no one, single, control center always directing activity. As Weimer points out:

> The person as a whole seems to be a *coalition* of hierarchical structures, somehow allied together but with no single locus of control. There is cooperation, but not determinant control, among the various mental systems. Clearly perception is not skilled locomotion, yet one cannot separate the systems in any determinant manner—the boundaries are intrinsically "fuzzy." Further, persons are superadditively complex entities; they are more than just the sum of the systems making them up, which is another property of coalitional structures. . . . The concept of coalitional structure allows us to understand both the unity of the person and also the welter of diverse systems that "go together" to make him up. 10

Because of this kind of structuring, the cortex engages in acts of both specialization and integration. Various areas of the brain have been discovered to be related to certain kinds of activity and not to other kinds. The dominant hemisphere, usually the left, appears to be concerned with language processes, for example, while the right hemisphere deals with nonverbal phenomena. But one must be careful about any conclusions drawn from such an observation. The cross communication between the two hemispheres is immense, and there exists in the right, or minor, hemisphere the latent capacity to handle at least some linguistic matters. The brain possesses a marvelous capacity to reorganize itself following damage, and to redistribute and relearn activities that have been temporarily lost.

We can observe the consequences of this kind of structuring all the time if we but look for it. To take only one example, sets of sensory neuronal impulses that appear to be very much the same in nature and action are evoked by differing stimuli and are experienced in different ways. Hence, we talk of touching, or smelling, or tasting, or hearing. Yet, our sensory capacities are interwoven in the brain, and subject to transformational equivalence. Thus, we create language phrases like "she could not swallow that uncomfortable fact," or we speak of the "softness of light," or the "brittle quality of his laughter." We are then reflecting more than just our ability to "author" clever or ornamental phrasing. With reference to comprehension, we often ask, "Do you see?" or we respond, "I see what you are saying." It is pertinent to note, respecting such imagery, that approximately one-tenth of the cells of the cortex are involved in interpreting visual data. This appears to make the visual the predominant sensory system in humans and to justify an examination of the visual system in our search for principles of sophisticated symbolic behavior.

Before we explore the visual, however, there are several more neurological phenomena we must consider briefly. From the description already given it is obvious that the mind-brain is capable of highly diverse activity, including handling data never before experienced. It is also clear that the mind-brain is active, not reactive, and there is an important sense in which mind-brain processes exhibit purposive and control functions. For explanation of these capacities, a theoretical discussion by Gerald Edelman is helpful.

Edelman proposes that the fundamental requirement for adapting to the vagaries of an unknown future is pre-existing diversity. Neurophysiologically, this means that there must exist in the mind-brain a large enough repertoire of neuronal groups that, "given a wide range of different input signals, a finite probability exists of finding at least one matching element in the repertoire for each signal."[11] Such a repertoire, says Edelman, must be "degenerate," by which he means there must be more than one mode within the system for recognizing a given input signal. There must be several or many cell groups that can activate to "recognize" the input signals. Further, there must be a high probability that such recognition will occur in a relatively short time. In addition to degeneracy and high probability of recognition, there must be "amplification" so that the perceived pattern can be "reflected on" and stabilized for future recognition. Amplification occurs, believes Edelman, because once certain structures are chosen for response to input signals, their chances for responding again when meeting with similar or identical patterns are enhanced. Amplification can occur positively or negatively; in other words certain neuronal structures will have their firing tendencies reduced. In either case, there will always remain other "unselected" cell groups which could be activated to the same input signal if need be.

One final process must be added to this already highly efficient operation. That is the process by which mind-brain constantly monitors both the external environment and its own internal state of affairs. This interactive, dual, reflexive monitoring process occurs continuously, so that internal mind-brain states can be modified in light of incoming messages, and the meanings of incoming messages can be modified in light of internal states. Such monitoring is made possible by the fact that at the various levels of neural processing, mind-brain can re-enter the "experiences" and "meanings" of internal states which have already been established, examine them, and use them again as if they were external signals. These processes are often referred to as "feedback loops," which are nested hypomorphically. That is to say, they are nested throughout the various levels of neural processing, with each level setting the aim for the level below. In the expanded forebrain of the human, then, there exists the neurological capacity for two concurrent operations; an analytical capacity for structuring information from the external environment into "meaningful" units, and a purposive capacity that directs and uses the structural meaning of the analytical system. 12 Edelman refers to these feedback loops as phasic re-entrant signals that occur in parallel processes involving associations among stored patterns and sensory or internal input. As Edelman describes them, phasic re-entry processes consist of two stages: a first stage in which processed input and its associated signals are held for re-entry into a second stage where a subsequently processed input signal is joined with the re-entrant signal and is associated with the response networks of both primary and secondary repertoires. 13 According to Edelman, it is this phasic re-entry activity that provides the capacity for what we facilely label, "consciousness." Because of it we have:

> (1) the ability to appreciate or distinguish different events; (2) the capacity to react critically to inner or outer states and to update information; (3) the ability to accumulate memories and to recall them associatively in temporal sequences; and (4) the capacity to distinguish self from non-self (self-awareness). 14

Hayek provides a slightly different description of the mind-brain's monitoring activity, but one that is consistent with Edelman's detailed explanation. According to Hayek's account, the ongoing activity and development of mind-brain results in the construction of what might be called a "map" of the structure of information that is significant to the organism. Hayek refers to incoming structures of information experienced in immediate space and time as "models," that are aligned with already established structures of the map so that similarity can be determined and novelty detected. The stability of the map insures the relative efficiency of "learning" and "behaving," since we do not have to cope anew with each incoming structure of information. While both map and model are always open to modification, the greater magnitude and complexity of the map means that modifications in its structure are not likely to be dramatic. 15

Hayek's account, especially, suggests a neurological basis for two observations which are a part of our contemporary, conventional wisdom regarding rhetoric and persuasion. In a variety of ways research on rhetoric and persuasion and common experience show that it is difficult to persuade members of an audience who are not already somewhat open to change. We all know how frustrating it is to try to negotiate points of difference with "closed minded" persons. We understand the importance of "mind set" in any suasory context. We are even led to say that we are only persuaded by our own reasons, or that the only successful persuasion is self-persuasion. The map-model relationship that sums up the activity of mind-brain gives such notions considerable support. The stability of the cognitive map which grounds monitoring activity would tend to assure conservative attitudinal modification.

On the other hand, most people are reluctant to conclude that rhetorical interaction is wasted effort or to deny that persuasive efforts can create the possibility for cognitive and behavioral change. One can find support for this reluctance at the most fundamental neurological level. Without going into all of the complexity of his discussion, I refer to the work of Eric Kandel. He concludes from his research on the relationships among habituation, learning, and small neural systems that there are certain synapses in the brain of simple animals which, though determined by developmental processes, are predisposed to learning and can be inactivated and reactivated through experience. There is a great deal of evidence that the human brain possesses similar synapses. If so, Kandel's findings "imply that even during simple social experiences, as when two people speak to each other, the action of the neuronal machine in one person's brain is capable of having a direct and perhaps long-lasting effect on the modifiable synaptic connections in the brain of the other."16 Thus, rhetorical interactions can lead to the modification of opinions and attitudes.

Edelman's description of phasic re-entry signaling and Hayek's discussion of model-map interaction confront us squarely with the problem of consciousness. In Chapter 1, I remarked that the nature of consciousness has not been satisfactorily determined. Some further attention must now be given to this problem because descriptions of mind-brain functions call for it and because all attempts to relate linguistic symbolic behavior to something called social knowledge, or explicit knowledge, or processes of explicit verification assume the presence of a state of consciousness.

In the workings of the mind-brain there are variations, gradations, levels, and continua of the phenomena we refer to with such terms as "consciousness," "purposiveness," "awareness," "intentionality," and the like. It is comforting to use terms such as these because they seem to give us something we can be discursive about, something we can get a grip on. The trouble is, the terms and concepts often prevent us from seeing that what we have a grip on is fluid; at a moment's notice what was out-of-awareness may substantially influence the experience of what is in awareness.

It surely is the case that we are able to focus ourselves in certain ways so that we attend to a particular phenomenon and apparently exclude other possibilities. At the sensory level we can center attention upon one object on a table containing many objects; our ears can pick up a relevant remark uttered across a crowded, noisy room; we can shut our eyes so that we may savor the taste or feel of something. These are not unsophisticated operations. No machine has yet been invented that can cut through an acoustically noisy environment to focus on one particular sound in the way a human can. At a more sophisticated level, we can concentrate our "thoughts" upon a particular intellectual endeavor to the apparent exclusion of other pressing matters.

But even at these commonsensical levels of mental activity, matters are not simple. We can easily alter our focus, or we can experience unintended shifts of focus, or realize that we are actually preoccupied by several matters while trying to give attention to one. In all of this we will be operating with habitual attitudes and behaviors that we scarcely think about, but they are related to our cognitive focusing. The tenuousness of "attention" confirms that the notion of a "unity of consciousness' is a comforting but deceptive fiction. As Ernest Hilgard put it:

> The first assumption is that there are many subordinate cognitive structures, each with a degree of unity, persistence, and autonomy of functioning. The concept of unity of the total consciousness is an attractive one, but it does not hold up under examination; there are too many shifts, as for example between the waking consciousness and the dream consciousness. There are also degrees of automatization achieved with practice, so that well-learned habits—such as playing a musical instrument, driving an automobile, or saying the alphabet—can go on with a minimum of conscious control once the activity is begun. It is important to note, however, that all these available activities do not go on all of the time or all at once; hence there must be some method in inhibiting them, on the one hand, and of facilitating them, on the other. 17

There are many activities we engage in that do not require discursive explanation in order for knowing to occur. Think of learning to ride a bicycle, or to water ski, or to ride a horse. Typically we do not receive a discursive explanation of "knowledge" about how such processes work. We may receive instructions concerning some appropriate behaviors and maneuvers, and we may observe others engaged in the relevant behaviors. But when we climb on the bicycle seat and put our feet on the pedals, knowledge *tacitly* held by our neurophysical system must operate in accord with principles of weight and mass, gravity and force, tension and pressure. With effort, we can explain some of this discursively, but the explanation will be cumbersome and turgid, and even when we get it rendered discursively, we don't "know" it as we know it when we are riding down the street.

It is well established that children know the principle of conservation before they can articulate anything about it, that we respond to certain kinds of subliminal exposure without being aware of it, though such response can later be called to our attention, and that our bodies can respond to emotions we are not at that moment aware of. Finally, neurophysiological research has shown that at the motor level the mind-brain

37

acts in accord with high level, tacit, abstract principles of function that take precedence over and shape all of the specificity we experience, but such actions are not fully understood.

What this indicates, I believe, is that to attempt to locate symbolic rhetorical activity, for example, in the realm of conscious activity alone is altogether too general to be meaningful. What level of consciousness does one mean? We face the same problem with such concepts as "awareness," "intention," and "purpose." What level or manifestation is referred to? And if we try to limit ourselves to discursive phenomena, or even worse, to language, then we arbitrarily disassociate ourselves from a great deal of the expanse of meaning and symbolic action. What we can do is trace what can be understood of principled perception and interpretation, and for this purpose the visual system is an appropriate system for examination because of its primacy and because of the relative wealth of research that has focused upon it.

THE INDUCEMENT ACTIVITY OF THE VISUAL SYSTEM

As I mentioned earlier, the visual sensory system seems a particularly appropriate one for survey because during the course of hominid evolution it became the dominant sensory system. The power of vision as a sensory mode has, in fact, the potential to override other sensory modes. For example, one can wear distorting eyeglasses that will make a straight rod appear curved. If the wearer is then asked to rub his or her fingers along the rod and describe what he or she feels, the subject will report feeling a curved stick. The subject is not feeling the rod in accord with the message the haptic sensory system is sending to the brain, because it will be reporting a straight rod. The subject is feeling what he or she is seeing. Why such a person does not "sense" a *combination* of the two sensory systems is a mystery. 18

There is much that is not known about visual perception. It is not known, for instance, how light that makes contact with receptor cells evokes a series of impulses whose frequency is related to the intensity of the light. On the other hand, brilliant research in the past quarter-century has revealed a great deal about the nature of vision.

We can begin by looking at a tacit, or out-of-awareness, function at the neurophysiological level, a function that is crucial to effective visual perception. The surface of the sensory system is the retina of the eye. From indirect evidence researchers find reason to believe that the operation of the edge of the retina is primitive and may provide some insight into the nature of prehistoric vision. Be that as it may, what is known with reasonable certainty is that the very edge of the retina is sensitive only to movement, but we do not experience anything when the edge of the retina is stimulated. Rather, a reflex action is started that rotates the eye so that whatever is moving is brought into the center of vision, allowing the highly developed foveal area and the neural network functioning in association with it to go to work. As R. L. Gregory puts it, "The edge of the retina is thus an early-warning device, used to rotate the eyes to aim the sophisticated object-recognition part of the system on to objects likely to be friend, or foe, or food, rather than neutral."19 Of special interest is Gregory's observation that the simplest and most powerful of visual sensations are brightness and its opposite, blackness. 20

Another of Gregory's observations is significant because it confirms that the visual system functions in accord with principles of the mind-brain. Some of the most exciting work on the visual system has been undertaken by David Hubel and Torsten Weisel. Gregory observes that among their findings is the fact that visual neurons are selective in their firing. Some will fire only when a bar of light is presented at a particular angle; when the angle is changed these neurons stop firing and other sets of neurons pick up the new angle. Still other groups of neurons will fire only in relation to movement in a single direction. Deeper in the brain are cells that respond to these characteristics in a more generalized way, and they respond regardless of which part of the retina is stimulated by light or movement. Gregory concludes, "Those findings are of the greatest importance, for they show that there are specific mechanisms in the brain selecting certain features of objects."21

Painstaking tests by Hubel and Wiesel have led to the most complete available description of how the visual system works. The cells that provide input to the visual cortex have concentric center-surround receptive fields. One set of these cells, called "on-center" cells, is characterized by excitatory centers and inhibitory surrounds. The other set is exactly opposite; it is characterized by inhibitory centers and excitatory surrounds. The on-center neuron's firing rate increases only when the center is bright and the surround is dark while the off-center neurons firing rate increases only when the center is dark and the surround is bright. If an off-center set of neurons is exposed to on-center visual patterns, its firing rate slows down, and vice versa. Under conditions of uniform illumination, neither set of neurons will be affected, and they will simply continue firing at their normal speed. Hubel and Wiesel explain that these sets of cells are particularly responsive to bars of light, or what are called "line stimuli." They are not primarily active in checking levels of illumination; their purpose is to compare the level of light in one small part of the visual field with the average illumination of the immediate surround. 22

When messages concerning light-dark illumination reach the visual cortex, the information they carry is rearranged so that the majority of the cortical cells respond to specifically oriented line segments. Here in the visual cortex, a hierarchical operation is effected. A simpler group of cells seems to respond very specifically to line position and thickness: "The response properties of these simple cells, which respond to an optimally oriented line in a narrowly defined location, can most easily be accounted for by requiring that the centers of the incoming center-surround fields all be excitatory or all be inhibitory, and that they lie along a straight line."23 Hubel and Wiesel point out that this kind of neuronal analytical scheme would account for the "strong steady firing evoked in a complex cell as a line is swept across the receptive field."24 They suggest, though once again the evidence is indirect, that cells sensitive to orientation may have evolved early and be associated with an early stage in the brain's structuring of visual forms. They ask, What cells at this early stage of analysis would respond to extremely simple visual forms? Their answer is that it would have to be only those cells whose fields are cut by borders or whose center is "grazed by a boundary."25

Here is a principle of no little importance: the principle of edging or bounding. Gregory expands upon it, pointing out that in visual perception a region looks brighter the darker its surrounding area, and a particular color will appear to be more intense when surrounded by a complementary color. He gives further significance to this principle of "boundary" or "edging" when he notes that it is possible to fixate an image on the retina so that when the retina moves the image moves precisely with it, thus remaining stable in relation to the retina. When this happens, vision of the image will fade after a few seconds. This raises an interesting problem. If one looks at a sheet of white paper, says Gregory, the edges of the paper's image move around on the retina, continually renewing stimulation. But the center of the paper could have no effect, because regions of brightness are substituted for other regions of equal brightness and there would be no change in stimulation. Areas of constant intensity would not be providing information. Yet the center of the paper does not fade away in our vision. What has to be happening, Gregory believes, is that such areas are "inferred" from the borders which do provide information. Somehow the visual system constructs the signals that are missing.26 This leads Gregory to conclude that "contrast enhancement seems to be tied up with the general importance of borders in perception. It seems that it is primarily the existence of borders that is signalled to the brain. . . ."27

Much work remains to be done in following the leads provided by the scholars. No one yet knows exactly how an entire visual form is constructed or analyzed by the brain from such bits of form as have just been described. It is not clear why there are two separate sets of visual receptor systems in the human system, with neurons that are activated in one eye only, but this is known to be the case. Neither is it fully known how the brain functions to structure color, but it is known that structuring plays an active role in perception of color.

Given what is known about mind-brain operation, it may very well be that the description of the visual system just presented is too simple. It portrays certain sets of cells becoming active to resonate with only certain kinds of structure and intensity, while other sets become active only in relation to other structures and intensities. It seems likely that sets of cells also possess multiple activation potentials and will fire differently when they form parts of a following pattern than when they are parts of an initiating pattern. Furthermore, the account presented here provides no map of chemical changes that may be occurring along with cellular activity.

The limited description so far provided does, however, yield action in the visual system that can be helpful in our attempt to understand symbolic processes and symbolic inducement. First, there is the principle that light-dark contrasts are searched for and made use of. Second, there is the principle of transformation that produces "edgeness" from data. By this second principle edges or borders or boundaries are structured. As Gregory points out, edges, borders, and boundaries are of fundamental importance to perception. Taylor suggests that while it is not the whole story, there is a sense in which each of the sensory systems may be understood as an edge detecting and edge producing system.[28] In view of the ease with which we transform the experiencing of one sensory mode into that of another in our thought and talk, it is not farfetched to conclude that the principle of bordering underlies all of our sensory-perceptual activity.

If the principle of bordering is so fundamental, it deserves further attention. The processes of bordering provide the contents of experiencing by stabilizing the ecological flux around us, and this is achieved through detection and creation of structure and form. Of special importance to our inquiry is the fact that bordering activity is an activity that is instantly symbolic. It is not copying experience. There is no experiencing but formed experiencing. To say that something is formless is usually only an acknowledgment that we have no handy label for what we are experiencing, but it cannot mean that we are experiencing something unformed, for this is a contradiction and a neurological impossibility.

Reserach on the visual system provides a strong base for believing that the processes of bordering are inherently a part of our nature as humans. We seem constrained to seek and structure edges and boundaries just as we are constrained to blink our eyes and breathe. In this sense such bordering is a *principle* of mind-brain operation. Doubtless it is a principle that can manifest itself in a multitude of ways within all of the patterned activity of mind-brain, and it can alter previous manifestations in various ways. However, though we can count on the bordering principle to be in operation, we cannot count on or predict the precise nature and outcome of that operation. As a principle of operation, bordering is a rule that guides behavior. But as Gibson reminds us, "The rules that govern behavior are not laws enforced by authority or decisions made by a commander; behavior is regular without being regulated."29 It is in this sense that bordering is a *principle of symbolic inducement*. It is a principle that leads, invites, and constrains our always symbolic, experiencing behavior. In other words, all human experiencing is constrained by bordering activity which, in turn, is not copying activity, but activity responsive to the holistic patterns of human experiencing.

Bordering activity *induces* other perceptual and interpretive activities, and it is always symbolic and present in all symbolic activity. But to say that is to be both true and redundant. The significance of the observation is that we must expect to find this principle of bordering or edging in all modes of human behavior and within all levels of human interaction. That means that among the places we should find the principle operative is the kind of activity with which this inquiry is ultimately concerned: rhetorical interaction and symbolic inducement. That the principle does operate there can be illustrated by examining the roles light-dark distinctions have had and still have in human symbolic systems.

It is generally accepted that at some point our hominid ancestors, searching for the ecological niche that would best offer survival, moved from the darkness into the daylight. 30 They had already developed an extensive neural system for the complex analysis of visual information. Undoubtedly the new interaction with the brightness of daylight further encouraged neurological development to enhance visual perception during daylight conditions. A sharpening of the powers of color perception might be an example here. In any case, as a result of the enlargement of the hominid brain, there developed the neural portions of the forebrain that increased the powers of association, coordinated and synthesized sensory information, and allowed the visual to become the dominant sensory system. This should not be surprising, for each creature that has been successful at the business of survival has developed a visual system congruous with the demands of its particular nature and environment. The frog's eyes are uniquely suited for picking up moving flies. The horse in its natural environment spends a great deal of time with its head down, grazing, because the digestive system of the horse works best when small quantities of food are ingested continually. In order to survive its predator enemies, the horse must be able to take flight at the first sign of danger, so it is no accident that the horse has a visual system that affords maximum vision (about 340 degrees) in the head-down, grazing position and is particularly attuned to catch movement. The human visual system is no accident, either. The light-dark distinction would be of crucial importance to the hominid. Survival would be optimally insured in the brightness of daylight and be most threatened in conditions of darkness. Further, research has shown that general body tone is raised by high light levels and that body tone diminishes in darkness. Apparently in consequence, our whole sensory apparatus seems attuned to the light-dark distinction; "bright" sounds and "dull" sounds, as well as "bright" smells and "dull" smells are known to be stimulating or depressing, respectively. 31 The light-dark distinction is thus heavily value-laden.

Symbolic manifestations of this fundamental structure can be found in human attitudes and behaviors across cultures and across time. Ernst Cassirer, for example, uncovered an abundance of relevant evidence in his study of mythical thought. Cassirer was not primarily interested in the functions of myths, about which there can be endless discussion and disagreement. He was much more concerned with understanding mythical thought, which he posited as an autonomous mode of consciousness, a way of comprehending. His discussion highlights the cognitive significance of the light-dark distinction. "In the coursing of the stars, in the alternation of night and day, in the orderly return of the seasons, man found his first great example of a uniform occurrence."32 More fundamentally, Cassirer noted that the mythical conception of space always begins from the opposition of day and night, of lightness and darkness. 33 Such early conceptualizations of space could, in turn, lead to developed notions of time, and space and time are knowledge structures fundamental to all human knowing.

Throughout mythical thought and beyond in the development of certain of its aspects into religion, the strong emotional value response to the light-dark distinction can be seen. The vast majority of creation myths, coming from many cultures, has the process of creation merged with the dawning of light. Another universal pattern of myth features the association of positive events and feelings with the East, the source of light, while the West, which swallows up the sinking sun, holds terror and darkness. The world of myth is also full of gods of the sun, or of light or brightness. Within this framework it is logical that the heavens should be placed above man, along with other things worthy, while such opposing forces

43

and beings as the "underworld" and devils and evils would be "beneath."
Man would "rise up" from magic to religion.

We could continue tracking across history, dipping into various cultures
for further evidence that the light-dark distinction is universal, but the immediate point is simply to establish the ubiquity of symbolization based
on the principle of bordering and one of its consequences, the pervasive
light-dark distinction. In our own time there are a multitude of examples
of the light-dark principle in operation. Observe that in India lighter
skinned people are held in higher esteem than those with darker skins. On
occasions of mourning one feels it appropriate to dress in dark, somber
clothing rather than in something light and colorful. We celebrate the permanence of values we hold important, at the Olympic Games, for instance, or at John Kennedy's grave, with the brightness of an "eternal
flame." We hear public leaders announce that social or economic or military problems are improving with references to "the light at the end of the
tunnel." The suasory impact of the light-dark distinction can clearly be
seen by anyone who bothers to look up the synonyms for "white" and
"black" in Roget's *Thesaurus*.

What is important for our purpose is that we are able to track a principle of symbolic discrimination from the neurophysiological level, through
ordinary perception and the working of mind-brain, to manifestations of
the same principle in structured symbol systems. The light-dark distinctions can be fundamentally linked to survival, to states of well being, and
to positive and negative value orientations. As a principle of symbolic discrimination, hence inducement, the light-dark distinction is a prime candidate for employment in rhetorical action.

Michael Osborn confirms the last claim in an essay in which he discusses one form of the light-dark contrast principle as it works in the light-
dark metaphorical family. Osborn observes that metaphors of lightness
and darkness abound in rhetorical discourse. He refers to them as "archetypal" metaphors because their popularity as rhetorical devices has en-
dured across the centuries and across cultures. Their hardiness is due, he
says, to the fact that they are fundamental to the way humans perceive,
think, and feel. They are grounded in prominent features of the environment and experience, such as day and night. Further, they embody what
Osborn calls "vertical scale motives"; that is, they tend to project desirable
objects above a person and undesirable objects below, thus seeming to express symbolically the human quest for power.

Osborn carries the appeal of the light-dark metaphorical family directly
to the level of neurophysiology:

44

Light (and the day) relates to the fundamental struggle for survival and development. Light is a condition for sight, the most essential of man's sensory attachments to the world about him. With light and sight one of us is informed of his environment, can escape its dangers, can take advantage of its rewards, and can even exert some influence over its nature. Light also means the warmth and engendering power of the sun, which enable both directly and indirectly man's physical development.

In utter contrast is darkness (and the night), bringing fear of the unknown, discouraging sight, making one ignorant of his environment—vulnerable to its dangers and blind to its rewards. One is reduced to a helpless state, no longer able to control the world about him. Finally, darkness is cold, suggesting stagnation and thoughts of the grave. 34

The metaphorical structures that feature the warmth of radiance of the sun or that picture images of heat and cold and the cycle of seasons belong in the light-dark family according to Osborn, because they partake of similar emotional states. Osborn says that such metaphors can easily evoke a sense of determinism, since they are rooted in a natural cycle that is inevitable and continuous. They may therefore be used as rhetorical strategies (albeit unconscious ones) to simplify situations and to associate the powerful emotional feelings they can evoke with attitudes or actions being offered for acceptance or rejection. They are thus devices of symbolic inducement, working to enhance or deprecate as the case may be. "Therefore," concludes Osborn, "vivid symbolic representations of light and darkness may often perform a subtle but fundamental probative function in a speech, well deserving individuation in such cases as *argument by archtype.*"35

What can we conclude from this part of our exploration? The light-dark distinction is fundamental to perception at the neurophysiological level. It is a specific symbolic activity that both illustrates and underlies the more general symbolic process of "bordering" human experience. Processes of "bordering" or "edging" are fundamental to human experiencing and behaving, so we should expect, and we find, manifestations of bordering activity across the spectrum of human symbolic activity. In the same fashion, we should expect other principles of mind-brain operation to actively manifest inducements in all symbolic forming.

BRAIN FUNCTION AND THE PRINCIPLES OF INDUCEMENT

We have seen that mind-brain is always active, always traveling at what we might call a "cruising speed." The motor centers of the brain, on their own initiative and/or in correspondence with phenomena in the external environment, coordinate the firing of various neural patterns within the

45

sensory system. These patterns may be described as distributive and degenerative; that is, there are various neural patterns throughout the brain which can be activated with regard to a stimulus, though they will not all be activated every time. Further, the brain operates on the principle of hierarchy; multiple hierarchies are activated within the neurophysiological system. Thus, information perceived by the sensory system will undergo a number of transformations before reaching a final destination. We must not forget, however, that information may also be generated within brain function, without originating at the sensory level, and perhaps terminating before reaching that level. Higher level hierarchical activity is more abstract than activity that occurs at lower levels, and higher level activity constrains lower level activity. Thus, in all cognitive activity there operates the principle of primacy of the abstract. Abstract brain functions initiate neural activity which leads to perceiving and constant abstracting and integrating of further patterning. There is constant monitoring both of external environment and internal states throughout this operation. While it is natural to consider all of this activity in a positive contributory framework, we must not forget that it is equally important to consider the inhibitory function of mind-brain operation. The facilitation of functions that structure patterns is achieved by inhibiting a multitude of alternative firing possibilities. Finally, it is to be remembered that, generally speaking, the firing of a particular neural pattern will enhance the potential for it to fire again under sufficiently similar circumstances.

The purpose of all this mind-brain activity is to construct a map of reality against which perceptual models of external and internal information may be placed for monitoring. Such modeling procedures allow for modification of the neural structure at any level of activity, but perhaps more importantly, the procedures give us the capacity to anticipate the future. Prediction of patterns is the ultimate goal of mind-brain activity, for if the organism is to survive it must be able to predict and modify its activity accordingly. As Weimer puts it, modeling as an activity of the central nervous system is a richer concept than "representation."[36] It is through the cognitive activity of thought that humans model their reality. But not through "conscious" thought alone, whatever we choose to mean by "conscious." "Indeed, *modeling is the fundamental function of the central nervous system*, . . . and it is exemplified in every instance of assimilation and accommodation that occurs in the life of an organism."[37]

Models are structures of assimilated and/or associated patterns which are composed of structures of information. Perception is never of an individual entity, but always of entities in relation to other entities so that it is the structure of the relationship that is abstracted for perception. The literature bearing on perception is replete with references to these structures and patterns. Rudolf Arnheim, pursuing his interests in the affects of art, says that the perception of shape is the grasping of structural features; "There is no way of getting around the fact that an abstractive grasp of structural features is the very basis of perception and the beginning of all cognition."[38] N. R. Hanson, interested in the philosophy of science, traces structures of information from the perception of a geographical entity to its representation in the form of a map of cartographic verisimilitude to its transformed representation on an aviator's navigational chart, showing that each of these transformations contains corresponding structures.[39] In geometry, the structure of information can be referred to as the "concept of group." Cassirer shows how groups comprise the various geometrical systems and demonstrates that they change as one moves from lower to higher order systems of abstraction, though some structural invariants are always present.[40] A number of studies of memory reveal that well organized or structured phenomena persist longer than the less orderly. Structure or pattern is a ubiquitous phenomenon in perception and cognition.

It is typical to want to separate sensation, by which we ordinarily mean the sensory reception of data, from perception, by which we mean the shaping of those data. But such separation will not do; every sensation is already structured by mind-brain. As the preceding analysis has shown, there are no data without structure. All of our reality, all that we perceive and know is structured from the beginning. This raises the question of what we perceive when we perceive something. Is there really an external reality "out there," or are we entirely captive to interior mental processes? In the latter case we make up our world as we want it. The questions obviously bear on consideration of such phenomena as "truth," "objectivity," "verification," and so on. I do not intend a major philosophical discussion of this matter, but given the evidence from neurophysiology and cognitive psychology, I hope to deal with the question directly and simply.

On the one hand, what we learn from data concerning visual perception argues against direct perception of reality. The visual receptors are attuned to perceive organized data, and those data are transformed a number of times before they reach the higher levels of brain activity. Ingenious research has shown color to be somehow constructed in perceptual function, rather than to exist in the data initially picked up.[41] This would argue for a constructivist position with regard to knowledge.

Common sense, however, tells us that there is, indeed, something out there. If we walk directly into a tree, we are going to get smacked and various of our sensory systems will deny the possibility of pure imagination.

Studies of visual perception in cats[42] and of humans influenced by illusions[43] indicate that the retina is clearly tuned to something in the external environment.

Let me be more specific. There is an external reality, and the human mind-brain is wired to interact with certain aspects of that environment, perceiving it in terms of structures of information which are the results of normal brain processing. We perceive what our neurophysical make-up is prepared to structure from the given environment. There are obvious limits. The reality of certain animals is filled with more smells than we humans are capable of detecting; yet other animals are equipped with receptors that allow far more night perception than we can summon. We humans are restricted in our ability to perceive sound. One conclusion that seems inevitable is that "reality" varies from species to species and is structured for each in accordance with the principles of its own neurophysiological functioning. In keeping with this conclusion, Karl Pribram proposes at least an initial answer to the question, What do we perceive? "We perceive a physical universe not much different in basic organization from that of the brain."[44] This does not mean that the human brain cannot construct a fantasy. It does mean that we do not live in a world solely of direct perception or a world of free-wheeling construction. One of the fundamental balancing acts of the brain involves coping with the interaction of these two realities.

There remains a most important aspect of mind-brain activity that is largely missing from this account. Recall that in Osborn's discussion of the power of inducement of the light-dark metaphorical family, he was conscious of the fact that emotions or feeling states are signficant components in suasory configurations. Despite the attempts of various "rationalist" schools to transcend or downgrade, and thus deflect our attention from, such "psychological" factors, emotions have always played a central role in human behavior. Until recently, very little sense has been made of the emotional system which must be an aspect of mind-brain process.

It has been known for some time that basic survival motives seem to be activated in the mid-brain, which is older in evolutionary development than the cortex. For this reason, the inference that feeling states generated in the mid-brain are everywhere present and have potential to constrain mind-brain activity appears plausible.

> We can . . . note the primordiality of the neurophysiological correlates of affective reactions. We know that the autonomic nervous system, with its organizational centers in the mid-brain is primitive neurologically and physiologically. It seems possible that affective meaning is intimately related to the functioning of the nonspecific projection system as it mediates autonomic reactions from hypothalamic, reticular, or limbic sys-

tems to the frontal lobes. Both are gross and nondiscriminative, but highly generalized systems and both are associated with the emotional, purposive and motivational dynamics of the organism. But there is more to it than this, we think. It is precisely because this affective reaction system is so generalized—can participate equally with all of the sensory modalities and yet is independent of any of them—that its gross but pervasive structure overshadows the more discriminative semantic systems. 45

While the inference is a reasonable one, exactly how emotional states emanating from mid-brain interact with other features of the brain's messenger systems is not known. And even if we did know, it seems unlikely that we would yet be accounting for more sophisticated emotional states, such as "pride" or "shame." Taylor believes that most of our emotions must be closely linked with cognitive factors, that is, with expectations of the future or with past experiences. 46

We may be entering a period in which we shall learn more about emotion. Neuroscientists have discovered and begun to explore the chemical message system in mind-brain. Until very recent times primary attention has been focused on the electrical messenger system. But the discovery of chemicals heretofore unknown and the concomitant realization that the chemical system is deeply involved with emotional states are leading to exciting research possibilities. What has already been learned reveals the mind-brain to be even more complex than has been thought. Peptides, for instance, appear to be major components of the mind-brain transmitter system, acting to keep messages separate and to channel their flow. Many different peptides are located in the amygdala, a key center for emotional arousal. Now, neuroscientists face new puzzles, such as the fact that two distinct peptides may reside in the same synapse, making it possible for a single cell to handle two or more messages simultaneously. One writer, surveying current discoveries, concludes that these newly discovered chemicals, obviously so prominent in the brain's operation, may carry the message "that the mind and the body are more intimately connected than we have thought." 47 The message relevant to my exploration is that we cannot now specify what factors pertinent to a study of symbolic inducement will emerge from discovery of the principles of the chemical messenger system in the brain. Nonetheless, emotion is surely a part of our total equation; we simply cannot be sure how to fit it in. Whatever the future holds, we shall probably find that the emotion-reason dichotomy is a specious one.

PRINCIPLES OF INDUCEMENT

We emerge from this part of our survey with some fundamental principles of symbolic inducement that deserve our attention.

1. *The principle of "edging" or formulating "boundaries."* We saw this principle at its most fundamental level in visual perception, where the basic operation is detecting light-dark contrasts. We noted that the principle is so important that the mind-brain will, in accord with certain visual cues, construct borders or boundaries where they do not exist and will function to complete discontinuous borders in perception. The same principle operates within the other sensory systems. 48 All perception involves interpolations across gaps in data. We should expect to find the principle of edging, or bordering, or structuring contrast to be a significant factor in symbolic inducement.

2. *Rhythm.* All mind-brain activity is rhythmic activity. We perceive data rhythmically, and such data rhythmically pulsate across the pathways of mind-brain. Like emotion, rhythm is all pervasive and must play a role in symbolic inducement. We shall find reason to give rhythm rebirth as a principle of rhetorical behavior, a matter for discussion in later chapters.

3. *Association.* The largest portion of cortex-mass, and corresponding brain activity, is employed in the business of associating. Several operations occur in relation to the larger function of associating, but contrasting and comparing are the heart of the matter. Hayek refers to the general process of discrimination, and to equivalence, generalization, and transfer, all of which are involved in structuring relationships of identity. 49

4. *Classification.* This is the outcome of contrast and comparison. At the most fundamental level we perceive "groupings," and mind-brain activity continues to function in accord with the principle of grouping or classifying at all levels.

5. *Abstraction.* The basic neurological act of perception is an act that structures by abstracting from the total environment. The continual activity of classifying is also and at the same time the continual activity of abstracting. Abstraction is positive; it helps achieve economy and efficiency. It is also a process of distortion. In all these respects it is a central factor in inducement.

6. *Hierarchy.* Mind-brain can be conceived as a network of nested systems of meanings composed of subordinate and superordinate structures of meaning. As humans, we do not tend to like loose ends; we prefer that things fit together in overall systems. This does not necessarily mean that we achieve one thoroughly tautological structure, for our experiences and meanings are often filled with inconsistency and contradiction. It does mean we are induced to take various measures to achieve closure and completion.

One might argue that to include these phenomena, which are inevitable in mind-brain function, as principles of symbolic inducement is to stretch the meaning of symbolic inducement beyond recall. But to launch such an argument is to adopt a distinction that cannot easily be defended. It is to assume that one can clearly separate the un- or sub-conscious from the conscious, the intentional from the unintentional, the explicit from the implicit, the discursive from the non-discursive. If we look at the way mind-brain operates, we must see that such distinctions will not do.

A second problem is more fundamental. The argument requires that one hold to a position that conceives of manifested forms of symbolic behavior as significantly different from, or radical transformations of, those processes and principles that are at the base of all symbolic experiencing, namely the principles of brain operation. This position is decidedly difficult to maintain if we remember Pribram's statement that we perceive in ways that are similar to the basic organization of the brain. Gregory, too, has arrived at the conclusion that while there does not appear to be an isomorphic relationship between brain patterning and perceptual patterning, there is a very close analogic relationship. It is his supposition that what have been referred to as operations of the mind are entirely based on physical brain function.[50]

It is my position that all cultural and social phenomena and all human experiencing are made possible by, and are shaped by, principles of brain operation such as the ones listed above. *Insofar as anything has meaning for us, it will have meaning in accord with these principles.* Meaning in all of its forms is generated in the human brain. Furthermore the principles are two-edged, even multi-edged. They shape meaning and in turn are used to further structure meaning. They are an inherent part of explanation, injunction, appeal, and exhortation. They will be found in all symbolic activity, and in all more or less formalized human symbolic systems. Logically then, the next task is to examine a typical symbol system for manifestations of principles of inducement.

NOTES

1. Richard E. Leakey and Roger Lewin, *People of the Lake* (Garden City, N.Y.: Anchor Press/Doubleday, 1978), 134–42.

2. For a thorough discussion of this matter see Philip Lieberman, *On the Origins of Language* (New York: Macmillan, 1975), esp. chapters 8 through 11.

3. Wilder Penfield, *The Mystery of the Mind* (Princeton: Princeton University Press, 1975), 19.

4. For more thorough accounts of the makeup of the brain see J. Brown, *Mind, Brain, Consciousness: Neurophysiology of Cognition* (New York: Academic Press, 1977); J. J. C. Eccles, *The Brain and the Unity of Conscious Experience* (Cambridge: Cambridge University Press, 1965); H. Gray, *Gray's Anatomy* (London: Longmans, 1973); A. R. Luria, *The Human Brain and Psychologic Processes* (New York: Harper & Row, 1966). For a somewhat less technical and highly readable account of mind-brain anatomy and function see Gordon Rattray Taylor, *The Natural History of the Mind* (New York: E. P. Dutton, 1979).

5. Friedrich A. Hayek, *The Sensory Order* (Chicago: The University of Chicago Press, Midway reprint, 1976), 185.

6. See David Hubel, "The Brain" and Charles F. Stevens, "The Neuron," *Scientific American,* 241 (September 1979), 45–53 and 55–65. The entire issue is devoted to research on the brain.

7. See Walle J. H. Nauta and Michael Feirtag, "The Organization of the Brain," *Scientific American* (above), 88–111.

8. Ernst Cassirer, *The Philosophy of Symbolic Forms, Volume One: Language* (New Haven: Yale University Press, 1975 edition), 76. The italics are Cassirer's.

9. Hayek, *The Sensory Order,* esp. 43–96. I am relying heavily on Hayek's description and explanation because they bear directly on cognitive processes. Though first published in 1952, Hayek's description is consonant with contemporary neural research.

10. Weimer, "Motor Theories of the Mind," 307–8.

11. Edelman, 56.

12. Taylor, 62–63.

13. Edelman, 74–95.

14. Ibid., 94.

15. Hayek, 102–31.

16. Eric R. Kandel, "Small Systems of Neurons," *Scientific American,* 241 (September 1979), 74.

17. Ernest R. Hilgard, "Neodissociation Theory of Multiple Cognitive Systems" in *Consciousness and Self-Regulation,* Gary E. Schwartz and David Shapiro, eds. (New York: Plenum Press, 1976), 145–46.

18. Taylor, 321.

19. R. L. Gregory, *Eye and Brain* (New York: McGraw-Hill, 1978), 93. See also David H. Hubel and Torsten N. Wiesel, "Brain Mechanisms of Vision," *Scientific American,* 241 (September 1979), 155.

20. Gregory, 78.

21. Ibid., 47.

22. Hubel and Wiesel, 154.

23. Ibid., 154.

24. Ibid., 155.

25. Ibid.

26. Gregory, 58–60.

27. Ibid., 80.

28. Taylor, 180, 181.

29. James J. Gibson, *The Ecological Approach to Visual Perception* (Boston: Houghton Mifflin, 1979), 225.

30. Harry J. Jerison, "Paleoneurology and the Evolution of Mind," *Scientific American,* 234 (January 1976), 90–101. See also Leakey and Lewin, 23–42.

31. Taylor, 64.

32. Ernst Cassirer, *The Logic of the Humanities,* trans. Clarence Smith Howe (New Haven: Yale University Press, 1961), 41.

33. Cassirer, *The Philosophy of Symbolic Form,* Vol. 2, *Mythical Thought,* trans. Ralph Manheim (New Haven: Yale University Press, 1974, Eleventh Printing, 96–104.

34. Michael Osborn, "Archetypal Metaphor in Rhetoric: The Light-Dark Family" in Robert L. Scott and Bernard L. Brock, *Methods of Rhetorical Criticism* (New York: Harper & Row 1972), 386–87.

35. Ibid., 389. Emphasis in the original.

36. Walter Weimer, "The Psychology of Inference and Expectation: Some Preliminary Remarks," in G. Maxwell and R. M. Anderson, Jr., eds., *Induction, Probability and Confirmation. Minnesota Studies in the Philosophy of Science,* Vol. VI (Minneapolis: University of Minnesota Press, 1975), 457.

37. Ibid., 459.

38. Rudolf Arnheim, *Visual Thinking* (Berkeley: University of California Press, 1969), 161.

39. Norwood Russell Hanson, "A Picture Theory of Theory Meaning" in Robert Colodny, ed., *The Nature and Function of Scientific Theories* (Pittsburgh: University of Pittsburgh Press, 1970), 233–74.

40. Ernst Cassirer, "Reflections on the Concept of Group and the Theory of Perception" in Donald Phillip Verene, ed., *Symbol, Myth and Culture: Essays and Lectures of Ernst Cassirer, 1935–1945* (New Haven: Yale University Press, 1979, 271–91.

41. Taylor, 204–8.

42. See C. Blakemore, "Developmental Factors in the Formation of Feature Extracting Neurons" in O. Schmitt and F. G. Worden, eds., *The Neurosciences Third Study Program* (Cambridge: MIT Press, 1974), 105–13; and H. Hirsch and D. N. Spinelli, "Distribution of Receptive Field Orientation: Modification contingent on Conditions of Visual Experience," *Science,* 168 (1970) 869–71.

43. J. J. Gibson, "What Gives Rise to the Perception of Motion?" *Psychological Review,* 75 (1968), 335–46. See Gibson's book, *The Senses Considered as Perceptual Systems* (Boston: Houghton Mifflin, 1966) for his general theory of direct perception, also his *The Ecological Approach to Visual Percpetion.* See also G. Johnasson, "Visual Perception of Biological Motion and a Model for its Analysis," *Perception and Psychophysics,* 14 (1973), 201–11.

44. Karl H. Pribram, "Some Comments on the Nature of the Perceived Universe" in R. E. Shaw and J. D. Bransford, eds., *Perceiving, Acting and Knowing* (Hillsdale, N.J.: Lawrence Erlbaum Associates, 1977); see also his *Languages of the Brain* (Englewood Cliffs, N.J.: Prentice-Hall, 1971) for his holonomic theory of brain processing.

45. Charles E. Osgood, William H. May, and Murray S. Miron, *Cross-Cultural Universals of Affective Meaning* (Urbana: University of Illinois Press, 1975), 395.

46. Taylor, 289.
47. Joel Gurin, "Chemical Feelings," *Science 80,* Premier Issue (November–December 1979), 28–32.
48. Taylor, 174.
49. Hayek, 17.
50. Richard L. Gregory, *Mind in Science* (Cambridge: Cambridge University Press, 1981), 565.

3

THE ODYSSEY OF
LANGUAGE

We humans are fond of celebrating ourselves. One of the ways we achieve a positive image of our kind is by contrasting what we take to be our sophisticated capacities and achievements and those of other forms of life. Intellect is an obvious target in these comparative exercises because other forms of life are superior to us in physical and sensory capacities. We cannot win at running or flying or hearing or smelling so we enjoy contrasting the intellectual capacities of the various species.

Among intellectual characteristics chosen for attention, linguistic attainments are cited more than any others to demonstrate our uniqueness; for example:

> On the one hand it [command of language] seems an unmistakable single thing. Like the clothes that mattered so much to Gulliver, you cannot miss it. It plainly calls for innate powers, which are linked to the main structural properties of our life. Human talk involved thinking conceptually, having a sense of things absent, being capable of abstract calculation, conscious of self, and all the rest of it. So we naturally see it as the key to our castle. 1

We proudly point to our linguistic achievements as being "distinctly human," separating man from beast, as the prime evidence of our singularly advanced intellect. Our veneration of the human ability to use language becomes so fulsome at times that we narrow our focus until we see language as central to all we do. Sentences like, "We know all that we know through language," or "All thought is mediated by language," slip easily off our tongues and pens. Though opinions differ on the matter, recent work with chimpanzees may give us reason to believe that we are not as unique as we thought with regard to language ability. Washoe and some of her fellow chimps have been successfully taught a sign language of the deaf and dumb called Ameslan, which they use spontaneously in interaction with each other. Having acquired the language they don't wait around for rewards, but go right on "talking" to one another as if it was the most natural thing in the world. They talk to themselves, they swear without having been taught to do so, and they demonstrate that they have self-awareness. One of the chimps (named Ally) was made familiar with both English and Ameslan and can accurately use Ameslan to refer to absent objects when their English names are spoken. This achievement, called "cross-modal transfer," was heretofore thought to be beyond the capacity of nonhuman forms of life. A limited physiological capacity to produce a multitude of sounds may turn out to be the most serious handicap chimps suffer with regard to language capacity. 2

Language need not be the only special feature on which to build an argument for distinction in the human character. We could choose to think of ourselves as the religious animal, or the laughing animal, or the reasoning animal, or the animal capable of contemplating the future, or the culture-building animal. But in whatever direction we turn, we are likely to find other forms of life that also possess the capacities on which we focus. Differences between ourselves and other species are likely to reside in the high levels of sophisticated development achieved by humans rather than in the uniqueness of human capacity.

It is the general capacity to symbolize that seems to set off the human from other forms of life. It appears that human symbolic capacity was made possible by the enlargement of the "new brain," the cortex and frontal lobes. The brain expansion occurred about the time it is thought that great ecological upheavals caused deforestation of huge areas of the world, creating treeless plains. Whether it occurred over time or suddenly, the expansion of the human brain was a dramatic change, and the consequences were phenomenal. The human became sensitive to a vastly increased array of stimuli and had to evolve the capacity to delay and integrate a multitude of perceptions over extended periods of time. Signalic systems of response became transformed into symbolic systems as the ability to objectify and evaluate experience evolved. Seymour Itzkoff summarizes these developments in especially relevant terms:

> It was during this period that man must have learned, perhaps painfully, to shift his behavior from an instinctual to a societal locus of control. The morphological potentialities of the brain are certainly responsible for translating man's inner thoughts into an external state and public form of behavior—language. Man's convenient capacity to vocalize and thus express symbolically his unique rendering of perceptual experience through meanings communicable to others facilitated the growth of cultural control. Thus the first phase of an adaptive shift was culminated. The second by which the symbolic realm itself began to be utilized for man's survival and adaptation, must be thought of as the subsequent use of a preadaptation, the primary purpose of which was other than a concrete organic response to an external environmental challenge. 3

Symbolic capacity produced new possibilities for experiencing symbolically, and these led, in turn, to the production of various symbol systems. All of these symbolic systems are open to scientific and speculative analysis. My concern, however, will be with the linguistic system. The choice is arbitrary but specially relevant to exploration of the principles of symbolic inducement. Language has received much attention; it is ubiquitous in human affairs, and scholars of rhetoric often place it in the center of their focus. Furthermore, compared to symbol systems such as formal logic or mathematics, language is especially flexible and open ended. As we learn linguistic meanings, we increase our ability to produce further meanings and combinations of meanings, and we do so in ways that are not predetermined. Thus, there is an important element of creativity in language systems that is probably not matched in any other symbol system.

THE BEGINNINGS OF LANGUAGE

The origin of language is shrouded in prehistory, and we shall never know what prompted the kinds of behavior that led the homonid to begin development of language as we know it. There is a particularly murky period in reconstructable history during which Neanderthal man disappeared and *Homo sapiens* emerged with a good deal of neurophysiological, intellectual, and cultural development already established and in progress. By the time earliest *Homo sapiens* is known to us, considerable tool invention and use was already underway and growing in sophistication, ceremony and ritual were established parts of life, and music, art, and other modes of symbol construction were in evidence. Language, too, was developing, influencing and being influenced by the total constellation of cultural achievements. Determining causalities within these developments is hopeless. Moreover, any attempt to specify causes and effects would probably result in gross distortion through reductionism. There is far more reason to believe that many developments occurred together across time and in ways that were mutually encouraging than there is to believe that any one factor was the cause of it all. For instance, the expansion in brain size was necessary for the kinds of intellectual activity that we are capable of today. But brain expansion did not happen instantly, and it is likely that intellectual activity increased gradually with the evolving brain and that that increasing activity gave added impetus to brain enlargement. Every ongoing experience of *Homo sapiens* must have had the potential to influence further neurophysiological modification. In turn, all such modifications constrained intellectual growth and maturation.

We shall never know exactly how or why human languages came to be. Nonetheless, some of the informed speculation on the origins of language can give us insight into the functions language performs for modern human experiencing. As we shall see, language was probably developed to aid human intelligence in ways that go far beyond simply communicating.

Mary Midgley offers the reasonable assumption that language would be a logical development in creatures who had already found it advantageous to communicate orally with one another. She speculates that perhaps the hominid needed to be heard over a long distance, or that some cooperative venture involving manual activity or tool use made vocalization a more efficient communicative instrument than gesturing.4 Acceptance of this assumption implies several more. It is implied that our hominid ancestors were, by nature, outgoing, expressive, socializing creatures. If so, communing through vocalizing may have been one of the earliest linguistic functions. There is also something to be said for Midgley's hypothesis that our ancestors had need to communicate at a distance. At some point in human evolution our ancestors moved out of the forests and onto the plains, and there adaptations of various kinds, including adaptations in signaling, would have to be made. But there is more at issue than this.

Clifford Geertz notes that there is evidence of tool use among smaller-brained precursors of *Homo sapiens*, precursors who could not possibly have had a developed language. Thus, Geertz says, cultural artifacts were preceding neurophysiological development, and activities associated with production of the artifacts may have spurred physical development, since tool manufacture and use require manual skill and, more important, foresight. The need for skills and planning ability would modify selection pressures so that the forebrain may have expanded in response. With the expanding brain came more erect posture, reduction in the size of dental apparatus, a hand increasingly dominated by a thumb, and possibly advances in communication and social organization and control.5

We should be cautious, however, about treating tool using skills and symbolic skills as acquisitions of the same order. A tool may be thought of as an extension of one's body; the tool enhances the powers of the body. It is an instrument for use and production. In one sense, language can also be understood as an extension of the self and can be said to extend the powers of self beyond the physical frame. But it seems to me there are vast differences between these two instrumentalities. One can completely disassociate oneself from a tool; one can lay it aside for future use, store it with other implements for safekeeping, hand it over to someone else whose task it is to transport it. Further, tools make their impact upon the physical environment, and the results endure over time. Not so with language. Vocalization is much more intimately a part of one's body and self than is a tool. It is highly unlikely that early *Homo sapiens*, for all of his developing wisdom, would have had a sufficiently sophisticated concept of self to be able to disassociate from inwardly produced vocalization in the way he could detach himself from tools. Furthermore, vocalized sound is ephemeral rather than enduring. In many instances its effects are much more unpredictable and ambiguous than are the results of using a tool. But most importantly, the materials worked with are of a different universe entirely. In vocalization the patterns produced are of expelled or inhaled columns of air, the functions of which are closely linked to rich inner states of experience, and these inner states are absolutely essential if the produced patterns are to have any meaning whatsoever. It may be that systematized language evolved from the same neurophysical constellation that allowed the development of tools and in return was partly spurred by tool use, but to equate language with tool use (which Geertz does not do) is to miss characteristics of language that are essential and distinct from those of physical tools.

It is precisely because small brained homonids are known to have used stone instruments that Eric Havelock rejects the notion that language use can be closely compared to use of tools. Taking into account the discoveries of anthropology, Havelock raises the question of what kind of selection pressures might have led to expansion of the forebrain. He sees the need for an efficient mode of communication as one of the keys, reasoning that foresight would be greatly enhanced by a communication system and that much intelligence and planning could not survive without a communicative symbolic system. He notes that evolution created in *Homo sapiens* a configuration of the mouth such that when naturally engaged the mouth could produce a wide variety of repeatable sounds susceptible to linguistic organization. What was needed, says Havelock, was development of an oral code that could be systematized and shared and, most importantly, imbedded in the memories of individuals. Such a code would allow preservation of information essential to the survival of the species. Memory, emphasizes Havelock, is central to the development of culture, and it was the requirements of memorization that prompted the selective pressures that accelerated brain growth. 6

Though Havelock's theory starts with the need to communicate, what he takes to have been the substance of communication makes it imperative that oral language become much more than a simple signal system. Language would have to be a sophisticated system if it were to handle the complex intellectual experiences of the hominid. As Havelock puts it: "The central role played by memory in the achievement of culture by man should alert us to the fact that the significance of language as a historical phenomenon does not lie primarily in its function as communicator: or rather, that communication is only half the story. It does not itself define the peculiar resources which are made available."7

Harry Jerison's theoretical explanation is more complicated and detailed than others referred to above, but it, too, places the function of communication in a position of secondary importance in the overall account of language and its uses. Jerison, like Havelock, searches for the factors underlying pressures that resulted in increased encephalization of the human brain. He takes us back some 350 million years when, he believes, there occurred the advance from aquatic to amphibian forms of life. Such an advance would be very demanding, yet Jerison notes that increased encephalization did not result from it. This fact leads to the conclusions that the advance was a conservative one, and that the earliest mammal may have been little more than a fish who could "swim" on land. Such mammals, only slightly modified versions of reptilian life, were active at night. Over time, this form of life gave way to modifications in which small nocturnal animals developed improved olfactory and auditory systems, and some changes took place in the visual system, all of which were suited to animals that were active at night.

It is believed these little animals used echolocation to identify sounds in space, and thus they were able to develop a sense for distance. Echolocation works through the principle of translating spatial information into a temporal code. But the echolocating form of life, moving about at twilight, would also sense visual stimuli from distant sources. Thus, the combined sensory systems providing data from the environment would integrate to construct the experience of objects in space and time. Only so could the experienced data be handled in an efficient manner.

According to Jerison, the next advance occurred when the small mammal moved into full daylight; with that move came the need for an improved visual sensory system. Jerison notes that a conservative description of the nature of the modified visual system would picture it as working according to the same principles as the olfactory and auditory systems. That is, the visual system would encode spatial data temporally and would engage in object formation. Their move out of darkness into daylight and onto the plains meant that developing primates worked with an improved visual system, but now their olfactory systems either regressed or ceased to develop and ceased to match those of other forms of life. As a result the developing primates had to cope with more geographic range than ever before. Other forms of life could mark their ranges with smells, relying upon olfactory "labels" to provide them with a map of their reality. Our noisy primate ancestors, lacking like capacities, had to rely on the improved capacities of their visual and auditory senses and on their vocal apparatus to structure and delineate their territory. Following their innate tendencies and acquired capacities, they would begin to systematize their vocalizing. Developmentally they would be progressing toward the struc-

60

turing of oral language, the entire advance being spurred by the need to make sense of the visual data they were now able to perceive.

In this view, from the very beginning language and comprehension are seen to be intimately linked. Such an explanation of language is theoretically elegant, says Jerison, for it explains the evolution of a novel development in relationship to the conservation of earlier adaptations.8 On the relations of language and communication, Jerison argues this way:

> If there were selection pressures toward the development of language specifically for communication, we would expect the evolutionary response to be the development of "prewired" language systems with conventional sounds and symbols. Those are the typical approaches to communication in other vertebrates and they are accomplished (as in birds) with little or no learning and with relatively small neural systems. The very flexibility and plasticity of the language systems of the human brain argue for their evolution as having been analogous to that of other sensory integrative systems, which are now known to be unusually plastic, or modifiable by early experience.9

Thus, says Jerison, "We can think of language as being merely an expression of another neural contribution to the construction of mental imagery, analogous to the contributions of the encephalized sensory systems and their associated systems."10 In Jerison's view, then, language systems developed because of *Homo sapiens'* need to know, and because of the ways in which that knowing had to be constructed.

We don't have to accept any of the above theories of language in its entirety, but we cannot ignore the distinct summative position that emerges from all of them. It is that language is somehow centrally involved with adjustive processes essential to the human organism's necessary integration of environmental with internal data and to the need to create and maintain balance among these data. In other words, language is involved directly with experiencing and meaning. In some respects language is handy for communing and communicating. But it is such a ready facilitator of social interaction of all sorts that we are prone to slip the social aspects of language into the core of its nature. Whatever its origin and purpose, however, language as we know it is not a simple system designed for efficient communication. Its very flexibility, ambiguity, and open-endedness mitigate against efficiency. Language, as it is known to us, creates misunderstanding; it allows identical linguistic features to be used to express highly divergent points of view; and it can easily be used erroneously. If more evidence is needed, consider the great diversity among and within the language systems of the world. Evolutionary pursuit of efficiency will not explain the existence of language. It is as if humans worked systematically to insure that simple, direct communication could not occur.

Our question now is: How does language *mean*? To find an answer we must consider the relationship of language to experiencing.

LANGUAGE, MEANING, AND EXPERIENCING

The search for the relationship of language to meaning is a quest of long standing, and it is not my intention to recount its history here. I shall be bold enough, however, to claim that two fundamental mistakes seriously retarded efforts to arrive at a sensible answer, and we have not yet completely escaped their influence. The first mistake was to equate a system of language with its written form. This mistake is so common and so easily made that it again and again slips by us, totally undetected. When we think of going to school to learn language, we often forget that it is writing we learn, for it is through the medium of writing that we most often improve our vocabulary in a setting of formal education. However, we were well on our way to learning language before we ever approached our first classroom. And our personal sequence of development repeats history; systems of writing came late in human history, and they were preceded by generations of life that survived without written language. A human is naturally a vocalizer and a listener, and language systems are basically much more dependent on the artistry of sound production and sound perception than on evolved elegance of written or printed sentences. As Havelock puts it, "The habit of using written symbols to represent such speech is just a useful trick which has existed over too short a span of time to have been built into our genes."11 He notes that our habitual confusion of language with writing could only arise because many of us take literacy for granted.

Historically, this confusion between mastery of letters and mastery of language occurred about as early as it could: shortly after the invention of the written alphabet. Havelock shows that one can find the mistake in the works of Plato and Aristotle, where the term *gramma*, which literally referred to an inscribed letter, was used instead to refer to invisible sound. He believes the early confusion is understandable, because invention of the written alphabet may have been culturally required before there was recognition that speech was made up of discrete units of sound rather than of a continuous acoustical flow.12 Thus, modern equating of language with the forms of writing has a long intellectual history. One consequence is that our understanding of meaning becomes mistakenly narrowed.

The second mistake follows from the first. There has been a tendency on the part of those who specialize in the study of language to narrow the concept of "meaning" to "linguistic meaning." They then search for the characteristics of meaning within the confines of the structures and forms of language systems only. Such an exploration easily disregards the fact that mathematics, music, and art, as well as language, are manifestations of meaning. Explorers then arrive at the conclusion that all meaning is mediated through language. This error was compounded during the heyday of behaviorism, when the idea that humans can only know what can be counted or factored guided research. In this tradition human subjects, asked to produce meanings for investigations, were often asked to recall, manipulate, or create finite structures of written language after being exposed to stimulus items which were themselves finite structures of language. While meaning itself was never confined by these tight strictures, the researchers' understandings of meaning were. As Steiner points out, this approach to meaning was a drastic abstraction that trivialized the relations between language and mind. 13 Dennis Tedlock puts the matter more graphically:

> Analytical linguists, following out the possibilities suggested by an already analytical alphabet, have "discovered" the phoneme, the morpheme, and the constituent unit. Structuralists, attempting to push beyond traditional linguistic frontiers, have "discovered" eidons, motifemes, mythemes. It is the habit of such reductionist thinking to imagine itself reconstructing, in *reverse*, the actual processes by which syllables, words, sentences, and stories were assembled in the factory of the mind.

Working this way, Tedlock concludes, "is like a mad vivisectionist, thinking he will at last discover the secret of life if the animal on the table will endure just one more little incision before it goes limp." 14

A brief selective tour through some of the analytical research can be illuminating. Hobart Mowrer was one who believed that language meaning could be accounted for by principles of conditioning, with the addition of the notion of mediated response. The transmission of meaning through language was possible because through conditioning the response to the significant could be transferred to a sign which could in turn be activated by the use of sentences. 15 Operating on principles like these, Osgood, Suci, and Tannenbaum constructed their semantic differential which became a vogue instrument for the measurement of meaning. 16 The idea underlying this construct was the notion that people acquire meaning through learning to make mediating representational responses to words. Since the meanings for many signs would occur through association with other signs rather than directly, meaning became tightly language bound in this view.

Some objected, among them Katz and Fodor, who proposed feature analysis for the study of semantic meaning. 17 Their idea was that the meanings of words could be described as bundles of features (syntagmatic, paradigmatic, etc.), and that one could get a bead on linguistic meaning by administering word association and memory tests to find out which features were retained in memory, thus appearing to play the most prominent role in meaning. A good deal of research has been done using feature analysis, employing recall following manipulated lexical changes, use of marked and unmarked forms of word pairs, varied temporal orders, subordinate and superordinate relationships, and so on. Some meaningful clues began to turn up. For example, Sachs 18 and Fillenbaum 19 found that recall of sentences reflected the semantic content of the sentence while syntactic structure and specific lexical items began to be lost. In other words, subjects remembered the meanings of sentences, but rapidly forgot the specific sentence forms. Hyde and Jenkins found that subjects had to process words for their meanings before other features such as frequency of usage could be remembered. 20 A number of word association and categorizing tests (shaped according to the logical operations of computers and other models), were administered, and it was discovered that humans are not as logical in organizing semantic relations as the models presupposed. 21 On such evidence one may begin to suspect that language and meaning are not identical.

Indeed, just such a suspicion had led other scholars to choose a very different starting point for the examination of meaning. Their idea was that meaning has far less to do with finite structures of language systems than it has with the conceptual systems of communicators and the specific contexts in which they produce langauge. On these terms meaning would depend upon the linguistic *and non-linguistic* referents intended within a particular context and on what the communicators understood about each other. All of these factors would interact, and a particular meaning would emerge from among a number of possibilities. This starting point is obviously more cognitively than linguistically oriented.

The cognitive approach to meaning has a long history, though it was shunted aside by advocates of behaviorism. Kant, Herder, Wundt, Humboldt, and Cassirer, to name a few, consistently developed their theories of meaning within the cognitive perspective. One important contemporary approach to the study of language and meaning was influenced by the work of F. C. Bartlett, who in the early 1930s published findings from a series of experiments on memory. His findings led Bartlett to conclude that memory involves a process of meaning construction. Subjects were given stories to remember, and at a later time were asked to recall the stories. Bartlett's analysis did not turn up anything that resembled features, or small units of any kind, strung together. Rather, subjects seemed to begin with an overall impression of a story; Bartlett referred to this recollection as something like an attitude. Working from the impression, subjects would create a schema that represented the story for them. Remembering, concluded Bartlett, "is an imaginative reconstruction, or construction, built out of the relation of our attitude towards a whole active mass of organized past reactions or experience, and to a little outstanding detail which commonly appears in image or language form."[22] Bartlett understood memory to be one aspect of a larger system of cognitive activity, all of which was involved with what he described as an "effort after meaning." He rejected both the Watsonian idea that meaning could be reduced to observable actions of the organism, and the Tichenerian notion that meaning was provided primarily by a context. Rather, as Bartlett saw it, meaning was the result of the organism's active effort to assimilate to its cognitive system the materials of a contextual moment.

Taking their cue from Bartlett, Bransford and Franks much more recently discarded the typical approach to memory research that tested with lists of individual words. They reasoned that holistic semantic ideas ought to be employed in such investigations. They reasoned further that holistic semantic ideas might often be represented by several sentences, not necessarily experienced consecutively. Their approach was to use integrated semantic ideas composed of four parts, each idea being presented in one complex sentence, in four simple sentences, in sentences in which the ideas could be presented two at a time, or in sentences involving three ideas at a time. Combinations of these sentences, along with combinations from three other holistic semantic ideas were presented orally to subjects. Then a recognition-recall test was administered that included some of the sentence combinations the subjects had been exposed to, some new combinations that were not part of the original presentation, and one entirely new sentence that included all four ideas, so stated for the first time. Subjects were asked to indicate whether the test sentences they heard were new or old, and to indicate on a five-point rating scale the confidence they had in their decisions. Subjects were most confident that they had heard the sentence that included the four ideas together, though, in fact, no subject had heard that sentence. Subjects' confidence decreased as the idea sets decreased from three to two to one. Bransford and Franks conclude that their data strongly support the proposition that people construct holistic semantic ideas by integrating individual idea sets.[23]

In a follow-up series of experiments Bransford, Barclay, and Franks went on to demonstrate that the constructions of descriptions that people produce from sentences presented to them contain more information than was contained in the sentences. From this the investigators drew the conclusion that purely interpretive and linguistic analysis could not account for all the meaning available to and constructed by listeners. 24 A number of other studies investigating various and related phenomena, including context, have followed and a consistent perspective emerges: Knowledge is not just copied sensory input; it is a constructive process involving the evaluation of similarities and differences and the representing of things in terms of their relationship to other things. New knowledge is constructed and assimilated to a person's total knowledge system. In short, what is learned and remembered is more than what was experienced. 25

We should note that the description of the processes of knowledge offered by these scholars, based on their subjects' interactions with various sentence structures, more closely resembles the processes of perception and the operating principles of mind-brain than it does the features of language systems. We are directed toward a perspective that finds the meaning of language emerging in accordance with mind-brain rather than the other way around.

I stated earlier that we know more than we can explicitly account for, and we certainly know more than we can say or write. The findings just reviewed support this. Steiner puts it very well: "Though it is polysemic, speech cannot identify, let alone paraphrase, even a fraction of the sensory data which man, blunted in certain of his senses and language-bound as he has become, can still register." 26 W. F. Brewer enumerates the following reasons for discarding the notion that thought and language are the same: (1) differing linguistic expressions can refer to the same thought; (2) the same expression can assume different meanings; (3) the struggle to find the right word indicates thought behind language; (4) linguistic paraphrases must be united by thought; (5) complex motor tasks do not require language; (6) visual recognition does not require language; (7) themes of discourse require underlying thought schemes; (8) nonverbal beings such as animals, the deaf, aphasics, and young children show evidence of thought; and (9) the behavior of lying requires thought underlying language. 27 Finally, when discussing the results of their search for the cross-cultural universals of affect in meaning, Osgood, May, and Miron state: "When we do find differences—what we have called either sub-universals or uniqueness—the question arises as to whether they are attributable to language or culture. What is impressive in our data as a whole is

the lack of evidence for linguistic determinism of differences in affect attri-
bution."28

Once again, let me refer to Steiner and the perspective we keep return-
ing to:

> Though it is, explicitly, a study of the conventions or necessities of rela-
> tion between language and "what is," linguistic analysis has taken little
> account of the progress made in our awareness that the problem of
> "truth" and predication is to a large degree bound up with the procedures
> of the human perceptual systems. These are themselves intricate combi-
> nations of neuro-physiological, ecological, and cultural-social factors.
> The lack of awareness is the more telling as there are many points of mu-
> tual interest. 29

On balance modern research on the relations among experiencing,
meaning, and language makes it difficult to believe that experience and
thought are necessarily linguistic. We need to say that, at most, language
is only one of many factors that constrain thought and behavior. But to
say this does not clarify in what ways and to what degrees language influences perception, hence thought. There exists a large body of evidence
from studies in semantics, persuasion, and perception that seems to show
language has some influence on how we see, hear, and think. It is also un-
deniable that some languages allow and invite the expression of numerous
differentiations within a general kind of experience while other languages
allow very little differentiation within the same pattern of experience. As a
result the languages might seem to dictate quite different descriptions of
the same experience. Thus, the Laplander distinguishes many kinds of
snow, the Wintu distinguishes many kinds of cattle, and the Navajo has
one word for both grey and brown. Such differences among linguistic systems could suggest that the users of different languages perceive differently, and the host of lexical differences identified by scholars in the tradition
of Edward Sapir and Benjamin Lee Whorf have led some to the conclusion
that language predetermines what its users can think and how they will
think. To the contrary, I have been arguing that perception and thinking
can transcend and precede linguistic formulation. To resolve the seeming
conflict of viewpoints we must explore relations between language and
perception more deeply.

Color vocabulary and color perception are topics with which we can
conveniently begin our inquiry because for more than one hundred years
there has been a running disagreement over whether there exist genuine
cultural differences in color perception or whether there are mere surface
differences of color vocabulary. In their studies of color perception Brown

and Lenneberg have made some sense of the overall body of research, and their findings are suggestive of how we ought to think of the inducement qualities of language generally. They discovered that subjects found it easier to remember what color to search for if the color had a specific name, or was one of the simple colors such as blue or red. As Brown and Lenneberg began to present delayed and more complicated recognition tasks, they found that codability, that is, the employment of color labels, accounted for the increasing amounts of variance in color recognition. They concluded that if a language is more differentiated with regard to a particular field of experience, the factors within the perceptual field are more codable than when available language differentiates minimally. The more codable the factors, the more easily remembered they are. In other words, there is a relationship between codability and a concept's availability for use. 30 The authors take care to note that they do not claim that a differential case of perception exists *because* of language differences. In fact, in a subsequent explanation of the findings, Lenneberg stated that the majority of "conceptual oddities" uncovered by Whorf and others could be found in some group within the American society. And he went on to suggest that if a particular concept does not enjoy high potential for codability, it still does not follow that the concept cannot be held. Rather, it follows that the concept is not conventionally used. 31

Brown and Lenneberg's idea of codability is helpful. Another way to state the idea is to say that if codability renders an idea available to recollection and use, then we are talking about a process of linguistic "fixing." Fixing is not to be confused with freezing, for nothing of a permanent nature happens in linguistic fixing. Rather, a certain kind of experience is stabilized through the use of language, so that it will be more readily called forth under similar circumstances in the future. Gibson describes succinctly the framework for what follows:

> The learning of the language code as a vocabulary should be distinguished from the child's learning to consolidate his knowledge by predication. He gets information first by focusing, enhancing, detecting, and extracting it from nonverbal stimulation. Later, the extracting and consolidating go together. Perceiving helps talking and talking fixes the gains of perceiving. It is true that the adult who talks to a child can educate his attention to certain differences instead of others. It is true that when a child talks to himself he may enhance the tuning of his perception to certain differences rather than others. The range of possible discrimination is unlimited. Selection is inevitable. But this does not imply that the verbal fixing of information distorts the perception of the world. 32

I only want to add a final thought to Gibson's statement. Verbally fixing information does not necessarily distort perception, but it can be directive of it. Insofar as it is, it will inherently bring special interests to bear. In this sense linguistic fixing can itself induce symbolically. We need, therefore, to examine this process in detail.

LINGUISTIC FIXING

We shall be misled if we try to understand linguistic fixing solely from what is known about the uses of written language, because writing is a secondary human development that arose out of long experience with oral language. We must therefore begin our enquiry with what is known, and theorize about how our species used symbols before written symbols were invented. From that base we can proceed to changes in experience that were subsequently induced when alphabetization and various forms of written language became available.

Fortunately, some understanding of the modes of thought prior to writing is possible, for as Havelock points out, "alphabetization was originally a function of oral recitation; the two were intermingled."[33] In Havelock's view, among the pressures leading to the invention of the written alphabet would be those that led earlier to the techniques for oral composition and presentation, namely, the need to make the processes of memory more efficient, to reduce the energy required for recollection. The written alphabet would not alter the modes of Greek thought immediately; writing would be the servant of orality and would first conform to the demands of oral presentation. Consequently, early written texts and fragments will more closely follow the modes of thought prevalent in oral culture than works of later literate societies. Lentz's work on the oral tradition provides further verification for the early subjugation of the written to the spoken. He found that much early writing was formulated for the purpose of being read aloud, and that while Isocrates appears to be the first to move toward a conception of writing as an end in itself, even his works were intended to be read aloud.[34] Basing their research on these premises, many modern scholars view the texts of the *Iliad* and the *Odyssey*, the early writings of Thucydides and Herodotus, and, in fact, the text of the *Old Testament*, as revealing modes of thought extant in preliterate cultures.

In addition, there is an ample supply of materials from all over the world that have been collected under the label of mythology. As a label mythology has an unfortunate accretion of meaning which can obscure the perspective we are after. When we think of mythic thought, we often call to mind notions of magic, of superstition, of archaic ritual, and of fabulous tales of gods and goddesses. Typically, such understanding as-

69

sumes distinctions between unsophisticated and sophisticated thought, between unscientific and scientific thought, between illiterate and literate thought, with the former bearing connotations of "primitive" or "savage." The assumed distinctions tend to be grounded in attitides of intellectual superiority which hold the "primitive" mind to be inferior and wanting in intellectual capacity. There is substantial evidence to indicate that such an attitude is fundamentally mistaken. The brain size of *Homo sapiens* has been roughly the same since the beginning of the Ice Age. Why, then, should we assume that the intellectual capacity of the Ice Age human was substantially less capable of cognitive activity than we are in our own time?

In an impressive work, Alexander Marshack has demonstrated that the notations and markings on bones and stone and cave drawings from the Ice Age are systems of time factoring, lunar calendars, and the like. When such marking systems are placed in juxtaposition to the drawings of plants or animals or other figures, the entire drawing is time factored. That is, if the calendar refers to the rutting season for particular animals, the animals are pictured as they would appear during the rutting season. The characteristics of plant life are delineated as they would appear during the part of the growing season represented by the time-factored notational system. Marshack personally examined a number of artifacts from the time span of the Ice Age, and from cultures in various parts of the world that could not have been in contact with each other. In those data he found confirmation for his theory of time factoring wherever he looked. The notational systems referred not only to gathering and hunting activities, but to such functional aspects of life as birth, sex, and death. Marshack noted that Ice Age "art," in addition to being time factored, had a "storied" quality, portraying events, individuals, and actions in which there are beginnings, changes, and endings. Such drawings and notational systems amount to early cultural accumulations of knowledge. They show that already some need existed for a system of symbols beyond those of orality. But more importantly, they reveal a cognitive capacity for memory, for making comparisons, for mimetic and kinesthetic understanding, for learning, for formulating relational concepts, and for working with a time-factored geometry.[35] "For us the important thing is the combined evidence for an evolved, modern, cognitive and symbolic capacity found in the earliest levels to the last. Though traditional categories such as magic and myth, aggression, symbolism, and sexuality are elements in the stories, the whole might more aptly, if awkwardly, be called a "cognitive-and-time-factored" use of art, myth, rite, and symbol."[36]

Marshack's interpretation has become generally accepted. What it means is that intellectual advances that have taken place between the Ice Age and our own era can have had very little to do with cognitive capacity but a great deal to do with accumulation of cultural artifacts and knowledge. The findings just reviewed have expanded opportunities for cognitive comparison. Thus, when we consider the mode of thought and feeling in so-called preliterate, mythic, or oral cultures, we should consider it as Ernst Cassirer does in the introduction to his study of mythical thought: as a "characteristic creative elaboration" [37] of reality, open to modification, but already containing the seeds for the further elaborations. In other words, we must remember that the brain of the Ice Age hominid, the brain which "experienced" in what Cassirer referred to as the "mythic" mode of thought, had the *capacity* to abstract, analyze, synthesize, and engage in all of the other cognitive activities that contemporary humans do. No doubt, from the Ice Age to the eighth century B.C. those *activities* underwent evolutionary modification.

The primary differences that are observable between the modes of thought in pre-literate as opposed to literate culture have to do with matters of distinction and abstraction. For instance, preliterate thought, as revealed by early documents, operates on principles of animation, contiguity, personification, and concretion. There are qualities of immediacy and universality present in preliterate thought that become eroded or lost under conditions of literacy. For example, early preliterate, or mythic thought as Cassirer terms it, does not draw hard distinctions between animal life and plant life, [38] nor is there a firm distinction between human life and other life forms. It is as if there existed a spiritual life force that infused all the phenomena of the universe. Thus, in early preliterate thought, there would be no inconsistency in believing that the spirits of one's ancestors could return to reside in the spirits of trees or rocks at certain ceremonial times of year. The early preliterate world appears to have been one in which concrete events and actions occurred, where important matters embodied themselves in the concrete. The world of right and wrong in principle, as we know it today, appears not to have been a part of mythic cognition. Rather, specific actions and behaviors were described as being appropriate or inappropriate within specific and concrete contexts.

The conceptual thinking of literacy tends to break up events into causes and effects, but in mythic thought the emphasis is not on these discrete units but rather on beginnings and endings. [39] Causality in the preliterate world appears to have been unlike scientific causality; in the mythic world causality is a matter of contiguity, a fluid matter. Thus, animals that make their appearance only during certain seasons are perceived as the bringers of the season. In mythic thought there is freedom of choice in causal associations, so anything can come from anything because it can stand in spatial or temporal contiguity with anything. 40 In our modern world we think of wholes as being composed of or resulting from parts, but in mythic thought wholes are not broken down into parts. A part is immediately the whole, it specifies the whole literally. 41 Mythic thought does not draw a hard distinction between words and significations; words are acts and words are things. 42 These modes of thought, operating together, justify scapegoating behaviors, or the related belief that to possess the fingernail clippings of an enemy or to possess his name allows one to control him. It means that during a ceremonial dance the dance is not seen as representing a god merely, but the dance is perceived as embodying the spirit of the god; the dancer becomes the god. Finally, in early mythic thought there does not appear to have been any sense of self-awareness as we understand it today. Rather, the individual was realized only in the wholeness of community and derived all substance and sustenance from the whole.

As the preliterate world evolved over time, the flexible unity of perception seems gradually to have become demarcated in terms of differing accents, and early steps in the cognitive process of creating distinctions emerged. Such cognitive activity, in accordance with principles underlying patterned neuronal firing, would tend to encourage re-use and further development of that activity. As Cassirer conceived and exemplified it, certain accents of value began differentiating various spheres of meaning and experience. Such spheres began to assume characteristics appropriated to them as fundamental differences, as between the sacred and the profane. These endowed accents could in turn be projected in concepts of time and space. Cassirer refers to such cognitive processing as "hallowing," and he says, "Hallowing begins when a specific zone is detached from space as a whole, when it is distinguished from other zones and one might say religiously hedged around." 43 On this point our earlier discussion of the fundamental significance of the border or boundary in visual perception becomes pertinent. In the process of mythic hallowing the principle of bordering is an organizing force; it would be the basis for early activity of discovering and constructing distinction.

If one follows Cassirer's explication of the development of mythic thought, one can see the cognitive consequences of bordering activity: cosmologies develop with their distinguishing directional characteristics, various spirits that are the projections of human thought and emotion come to populate the various sectors of the cosmology, and differentiation proceeds to the point where numerical specification begins to occur. But there is a clear difference between the quality of the activity in preliterate or mythic society and that which would develop following the invention of the written alphabet.

Prior to possessing a written alphabet, humans' primary means of stabilizing knowledge and preserving it for future reference or for coming generations was oral utterance. Orality would come to the fore rather than drawing or notation or sculpting or other mechanical modes of structuring meaning because of the ease of producing speech, its versatility, and its portability. Havelock notes that "myth" is a term often used to denote the conventional oral behavior that was so important in cultural construction, preservation, and transmission. He himself prefers "epic" as a more suitable designation, in that "epic" is more comprehensive in meaning and better indicates the oral genius of the tribal encyclopedia which is at the heart of any oral culture. 44 Whatever term we choose, the central point is that wherever there is sociality there must be preservation of knowledge. Social construction, preservation, and transmission in any social system is bound to be patterned in some fashion, else it cannot be shared from one time to another. In a culture entirely oral or predominantly oral these patterns prove to be stylized and conventional, not ingeniously varied. The explanation usually given for that fact is that ideas so formed would be readily remembered, repeated, and preserved in a stabilized and stabilizing fashion. But early forms of these sorts could not have come into being had they not also been forms consonant with the cognitive principles that underlie perception and experience of meaning. And the earliest oral forms about which we have knowledge are in fact forms that reflect the kind of preliterate perception and interpretation that has been hypothesized in preceding paragraphs. Concrete events and acts are vivified and remembered by means of stylized verbal forms that "record" and hence fix patterns of "primitive" distinguishing, projecting, differentiating, and associating. What Havelock calls "epic" form had just such features. The entire enterprise would be a conserving exercise, with the stylized forms of oral presentation conforming to the extant modes of thought, and acting to further stabilize and fix those modes.

The mode of knowledge which meets the requirements of the memorized epic can be characterized in three ways, and Havelock enumerates them as follows. First, without exception, all of the events or data must be time-factored, that is, they must be stated as events in time. They will not be structured in a syntax that indicates "truth for all situations" and thus be rendered time-less. The data will be cast in the language of specific and

73

concrete doings and happenings. Second, events and data will be "unitized" in a series of linked but disjunct episodes such that action succeeds action in a kind of chain. Each disjunct episode will be complete and satisfying in itself. Third, the episodes will also contain a high level of visual suggestion, so that in the mind's eye persons will be vividly seen to perform behaviors. 45 "Thus," summarizes Havelock, "the memorized record consists of a vast plurality of acts and events, not integrated into chained groups of cause and effect, but rather linked associatively in endless series. In short, the rhythmic record in its very nature constitutes a 'many' it cannot submit to that abstract organization which groups 'manys' into 'one.' "46

We should notice that from the requirements of form listed above, syntax would much more readily conform to the structure of narrative than to any structure of analysis. Havelock points out that "oral storage is unfriendly to what we might call an 'is' statement; that is, it is unfriendly to the use of the verb 'to be,' or its equivalent in whatever tongue is in question, used simply as the verb 'to be,' meaning either essence or being, either what is logically true or metaphysically existent."47 He elaborates further, that timeless laws or principles or rules would not find expression in oral performance, nor would cause and effect relationships structured in analytical form. Havelock does not argue that the citizens of oral culture could not think in abstractions, but his point is that the pressures to economize and standardize the processes of memory would not lend themselves to stabilizing or fixing data according to such modes of thought. 48 Actions, actors, and events are most easily vivified for recollection by speaker and audience alike. In short, the early verbal forms of which we know conserve both what we presume to have been the character of preliterate perception and thinking and syntactical structures favorable to remembrance.

The most important feature of early oral presentation is what the father of oral-culture scholarship, Milman Parry, referred to as the "formula." This term refers to the grouping of words in accord with rhythmic patterns regularly employed. 49 Havelock suggests that rhythmic formulas provided "standardized incantations" that would be relatively immune to modification over time. Thus formulas could act as oral analogues to documentation in a literate society. 50 Rhythmical patterns of sound and regularity in cadence would not only serve to induce memory in standardized ways, but their potency would be further enhanced by the sheer pleasures of rhythmic production; even parts of the body could feel the invitation to participate in the rhythmic pattern. 51 One's entire being might participate in reinforcing ways to facilitate the mental task of memory. For speaker and listener rhythm could in these ways encourage joint participation, indeed immersion, in the act of oral production which more prosaic forms could never achieve. And we should remember that at bedrock level, the potency of rhythm for inducing animation and certain kinds of cognitive activity rests on the fact that rhythmic activity is a fundamental feature of the human neurophysiological system.

Rhythm could not only play a role in constraining sound production and bodily movement, but it could shape language use and meaning as well. Alliteration and assonance at the acoustic level would suggest analogues at the level of meaning, in the forms of antithesis and parallelism. As Robb says, "the mind is aided in the act of recall by the fact that something in the first member of a balanced pair suggests, or leads the memory on, to something parallel (or opposite) in the second member."52 Alfred Lord, who studied the oral tradition in Yugoslavia, corroborates Robb's claim, finding that wherever possible the singer "moves in balances: from boots to cap, from a sword on the left side to powder box on the right."53 Rhythmic fixing, then, becomes a functional part of experiencing and meaning. In a provocative statement, Havelock suggests the pervasive influence of rhythmic patterns across the various areas of Greek cultural achievement:

> The condition of communication had an effect which, so it could be argued, showed itself in the field of the visual arts, not *vice versa*. Was the protogeometric style in painting initially a psychological reflex of that severe training in acoustic patterns which the business of daily living and listening required? The patterns of the *Iliad* have been treated as though they were a visual arrangement, contrary to the premise that the composition was oral, and have been compared to the visual arrangements in geometric pottery. Is it not more proper to view them as patterns built on acoustic principles which exploit the technique of the echo as a mnemonic device? If so, then the visual geometry of the plastic artist might be a reflex in himself of that acoustic instinct now transferred to the sphere of vision, and not *vice versa*.
>
> This exploitation can stand as debatable, but it conforms to the established fact that in the Classical Age the specific genius of the Greeks was rhythmic. What we call the Greek sense of beauty in architecture, sculpture, painting, and poetry, was more than anything else a sense of elastic and fluid proportion. This faculty, presumably shared to a degree by all races, was, we suggest, in the special Greek case perfected by an unusual degree of exercise in acoustic, verbal and musical rhythms during the Dark Age. It was the popular mastery of the shaped word, enforced by the needs of cultural memory, which brought the Greeks to a mastery of other kinds of rhythm also. Their supposed disadvantage in the competition for culture, namely their non-literacy, was in fact their prime advantage.54

Let us be sure to place the importance of rhythm in its proper context. When we say that the pressures of memorization required the use of such rhythmic features of experience as balance and opposition, we are not saying that they were the necessary and sufficient causes of such modes of thought. Indeed, these modes are natural principles of thought that underlie the production of meaning in general. The point to be seen is that the rhythmic processes of oral presentation would serve to make such modes of thought more stable, fixing them in rhythmic pattern. The result would be to induce such modes in the further service of experiencing. Thus, the interaction of mutual influence would act to confirm itself, and such is the tendency with all modes of symbolic fixing. The proof that the oral modes of fixing did not amount to freezing lies in the fact that certain characteristics of the rhythmic formulas would atrophy from disuse when they were no longer needed. But the fundamental modes of thought fixed by them would remain operative and through transformation would occur when the written alphabet came upon the scene. In principle, what was fundamental remained constant.

It is generally accepted that the alphabet, which is second nature to those of us in Western culture today, was invented sometime in the second half of the eighth century B.C. 55 To be sure, systems of writing and notation already existed at the time of the Greek alphabetical revolution, but those systems attempted to link thoughts with appropriate shapes and were cumbersome and uneconomical. These systems would gain in economy as they moved away from their rather literal attempts at representation toward a more limited effort to represent only the acoustic sounds of linguistic orality. But even so, the early systems remained inconvenient and inflexible; they were in a very real sense over-productive because, in addition to signs for vowel sounds, they also included signs to represent the vocalic breath which must be used to produce consonants orally. The Greek act of reflective genius was to recognize that a vocal linguistic unit consisted of vibrating columns of air which were initiated and terminated by the action of teeth, tongue, lips, and palate. As Havelock describes it, the idea of dividing the linguistic utterance into its two theoretical components, then isolating the non-sound of the consonant and giving it its own conceptual identity to be affirmed by its own sign, was an intellectual abstraction that went beyond empiricism and language. 56 It is not surprising that the characteristics of the written language, birthed by an act of abstract intellect, would offer themselves as prime candidates for the honor of best typifying what is human. When the "magic" of writing is joined to and extends the preliterate veneration of the ability to produce words, the celebratory potential of language becomes formidable indeed.

The Greek invention at last allowed development of a system of writing that met the requirements for easy, efficient reading. Writing could now be used to trigger memory of all the distinctive sounds in the language, the triggering function could be performed unambiguously, and the total number of signs needed could be strictly limited so that memory was not overburdened. In addition the signs could be combined in endless ways, and so accommodate the flexibility and creativity inherent in the language system and in the processes of mind-brain.

The influences of written language on modes of thought begin with the reduction of mental effort needed for memorization. The ability to preserve thoughts and instructions in writing meant that one could loosen or even cast off the binding constraints of oral formulas that required a careful systematizing of words with rhythms. It was now possible to redirect one's cognitive energy in directions that the constraints and pressures of orality had left untried. 57 Preserved meaning took new forms; evanescent acoustical sounds could now be replaced by texts in material form, and these become objects rather than actions. A new kind of cultural artifact took its place among other phenomena in the environment, and it induced experiencing in particular ways that had neither existence nor force before there was writing.

Although the signs of the written alphabet referred to articulated sounds, they required that the visual sense become active in pursuit of meaning, and in ways that that sense had not been used before. Now entire messages stood still for examination. One could begin at the beginning or start a perusal anywhere in a message. One could jump back and forth, examining the parts of a message, observing similarities and differences, noting relationships, detecting discrepancies. Not only would messages hold still, but their parts could be moved around and new combinations of meaning could be created. We who are heavily steeped in literate experience cannot appreciate the feelings of power and control that must have been experienced by early Greeks. Now there came into being what Havelock calls the "architecture of language," that is, the patterns and structures of written tests, topics, subjects, themes, characters, and all the rest of the apparatus we associated with literature:

> As storage speech became an artifact, the eye if it chose could exercise upon it the kind of architectural expectation to which it had long become accustomed. Language as it presented itself to be read became a physical material amenable to an arrangement which was structural—or "geometric," if that term is preferred. This meant rearrangement, for whereas the previous need for oral memorization had favored sequences governed by the laws of sound, it was now possible to supplement these by

dispositions suggested by the laws of shapes. This is a theoretically bald way of stating a process which was psychologically subtle and lay below the level of conscious purpose. The eye joined partnership with the ear, as it has ever since, but did not replace it. 58

In addition to efficient preservation of ideas, allowing leisure for inspection and possibilities for modifying and creating new meaning patterns, written language encouraged perception of distance between humans and words. No such distancing was attainable under conditions of orality. Not only could written words be separated from the parties who produced them, but one could examine what one had produced oneself. Thus, a new level of objectivity became possible in the environment of linguistic meaning. That was, perhaps, the crucial accomplishment of the Greek alphabet, for achievement of linguistic "distancing" brings with it inducement to engage in cognitive processes we have come to know as "rational." The written alphabet did not create those processes. They were already operable and operating in the mind-brain. What writing did was to encourage them to become vital in experiencing.

Jack Goody points out that in the first fifteen hundred years of documented history, lists of various kinds dominate in typical verbal artifacts. There were king lists which would become important by way of providing data that aided transformation of mythic tales into history. There were administrative lists, business and household ledgers, event lists, object lists, burial lists, shopping lists, future itinerary lists, and so on. Some of the lists seem to have been carefully thought out, but others appear to have been experimental and perhaps the outcomes of playing around with the words to see what the results would be. It is difficult to know exactly what explorations in thought and feeling might have been guiding such experiments in listing, but listing was plainly a very early, favorite use of the new technology called writing.

We earlier established that the search for edges, the structuring of boundaries, the principle of bordering, is fundamental to cognitive processing. Linguistic fixing, of course, is a manifestation of the principle. Listing is an exercise in such discriminative fixing. In support of this, it is interesting to observe that Goody goes to the third meaning of "list" given in the *Oxford English Dictionary* to identify the important characteristic of the early lists. That third definition refers to the "the border, edging, strip, selvage of cloth." It is the function of defining a boundary that Goody has in mind:

> The list relies on discontinuity rather than continuity; it depends on physical placement, on location; it can be read in different directions, both sideways and downwards, up and down, as well as left and right; it has a clear-cut beginning and a precise end, that is a boundary, an edge,

like a piece of cloth. Most importantly, it encourages the ordering of the items by number, by initial sound, by category, etc. And the existence of boundaries, external and internal, brings greater visibility to categories, at the same time as making them more abstract. 59

We could not ask for a better description of linguistic fixing. Listing amplifies such things as distinctions, similarities, groupings, and relationships, and it amplifies in a way that invites attention and reflection. It also removes words and the items they refer to from active contexts and casts them forth in stable abstraction. It encourages cognitive capacities that spot inconsistency and contradiction. In sum, it induces and encourages the kinds of probative attitudes that lead to questions regarding what is and what is not the case. Here we begin to grasp the seminal significance of writing as symbolization. Writing would fecundate the cognitive principles embodied in the process of listing in such a way that notions of permanent and autonomous truths would be entertained. More than this, the incipient principles of dividing, comparing, defining, and relating would eventually suggest procedures for discovering, establishing, and demonstrating truths. 60

Aristotle would help to fix such principles as he worked out his systems of demonstration and alternative modes of proving and testing. There was plenty of raw material for Aristotle to work from because early Greek philosophical and epistemological discussion was characterized by argument from opposition. The principle of opposition was a natural reflection of a mode of perception tuned to the discovery and structuring of edges playing upon an environment which provided phenomena to be experienced in forms such as day and night, hot and cold, hard and soft, male and female, and so on. Such perceptions and cognitive experiences provided principles which by extension would undergird forms of talk and disputation. Lloyd reminds us that prior to Aristotle, division constituted the most prevalent attempt to construct demonstrations of proof. 61 Socrates, in Plato's *Meno* and *Phaedrus*, illustrates the point. Debates were often conducted from grounds of extreme opposition, conveying the impression that decisions could be made only by choosing between two opposing alternatives. It was not unusual for partisans of one position to refuse to grant any credence whatever to the opposition, or for them simply to ignore the claims of others altogether. These simple antithetical structurations provided ways by which complex matters were defined and categorized. They were instruments for achieving comprehensiveness and clarity, although they greatly distorted complexity.

Development of Greek philosophy led to recognition of more complex distinctions among categories of things. Lloyd points out that Democritus

79

had a finer honed appreciation of the boundary line between animate and inanimate phenomena than did Thales. 62 The sharpening of distinctions and their multiplicity pervaded the world of Greek intellect by the end of the fifth century, providing the climate in which Aristotle, following cues from Plato, could become interested in articulating general laws of thought. In the works of Plato and, especially Aristotle, we have examples of Greek intellectual development in this regard, and it occurred within two generations. Plato, in the *Phaedrus*, extols the virtues of his method of demonstration which relied upon definition and division. 63 Aristotle, writing later in his *Posterior Analytics*, argued that the method of definition and division was inadequate, and he proceeded to develop his more complex system of logical analysis. 64

By Aristotle's time, the natural proclivities of the human intellect were strongly aided by the fixative and preservative nature of the written language—a technology that had still worried Plato. Aristotle took friendly advantage of the new symbology. By enabling accumulation of groupings and distinctions, and by holding them still for examination, the definitional and bordering potentialities of written symbolization enhanced and extended the defining and bordering activities and potentialities of the mind. These possibilities Aristotle advanced.

Two overly simplistic principles of thought became candidates for transformation. The first was the tendency to regard any opposites as mutually exclusive and exhaustively alternative. The second was the tendency to assimilate similarities to complete identity. The latter tendency, still revealing some of the characteristics of mythic thought, manifested itself in the assumption that two cases which had some similar characteristics could form the bases for analogical argument constituting proof, without regard for the importance of existing differences between the cases. One of the significant contributions of Aristotle constituted a singular advance in knowledge in fourth-century Greece. It was his analysis and specification of the logical relationships of identity, similarity, and the different forms of opposition. A new technical terminology arose to help stabilize the relationships; terms such as "other," "like," "same," "different," "contrary," and "contradictory" assumed new importance within the developing system of logical thought. 65 Such terms and the concepts they represented give evidence that Aristotle and other Greek thinkers had moved beyond the predominant modes of thought in oral cultures that featured actor-action-event sequences. Without such a move, the tests of probity and the systems of demonstration would not have been developed. What we see in Aristotle's work is a change in perception, interpretation, and meaning that was encouraged and induced by the new manner of symbolizing which held ideas still so their cognitive ramifications could be discovered, explored, and further developed.

Terms such as "other," "like," and "same" not only helped to stabilize or fix logical relationships, but they encouraged the creation and elaboration of abstraction as well, for to say that three or four events or actions are alike in some way is to move out of the contexts of the events themselves and take a step up in the process of generalization. The potential for abstraction already existed, of course, in the species' cognitive repertoire, but like systematic logic, it required encouragement from the right mixture of environmental and internal forces. Havelock shows us an early stage of abstracting activity in Hesiod's *Works and Days*. Hesiod dealt with five familes of mankind which he conceived of in order to demonstrate typologies of moral conduct. In his treatment, Hesiod found it helpful to identify the families with a *logos* that was representative of a certain moral condition. Here, says Havelock, we see:

> how a vocabulary of the semi-abstract grows out of epic concreteness, not by substituting new words for old, but by altering the syntax in which the old words are found. It is the conjunction of the word "family" with the word for "strife" that first prompts the suggestion that a family is now being used in a rather special metaphorical sense. In this way all abstractions advanced by exploiting the resources of metaphor. 66

While many scholars agree that abstract thought was one of the major epistemological advances of fourth-century Greece, it is Havelock who provides an in-depth case study. He chooses to exemplify the general development of abstraction by tracing the concept of "justice" from its meaning in Homeric texts to its final transformation as a principle in the work of Plato. In the *Iliad* and the *Odyssey* justice was not a principle; it was, rather, a procedure established through negotiation between contending parties and administered by kings or magistrates. The administration of justice was a way of reestablishing proprieties in human relationships. Justice was always negotiated and administered within a specific context which featured specific actions. However, the seeds of abstraction lie in the use of adjectival extensions which make justice an attribute of a person. 67

Hesiod advanced abstraction as he tried to construct a field of meaning by separating different occurrences of justice from their narrative contexts and examining their natures together. The result was the development of an impersonal subject. Hesiod personifies justice as a goddess and refers to it as "her," a move that begins to differentiate the idea of justice from the action which administers it. But the ultimate conceptualization of justice as abstract principle awaited development of the impersonal pred-

81

icate. The written alphabet, says Havelock removed the pressure of memorization and provided the impetus for such development. When the needs for vivifying narrative form diminished, attributes could be referred to without embodying them in agents acting in relation to other agents. Subjects and objects could be referred to in nonpersonal ways. Equally important, says Havelock, connecting verbs no longer needed to refer to situations in time; they could be used to create relationships in logic which transcended time. In particular, the use of the copula "to be" could develop and grow. 68 The syntax of abstraction with regard to "justice" became full blown in Plato's *Republic* where justice is a linguistic constant, always representing a single thing. It is frequently placed in formal antithesis to its negative, and lexical devices are employed which refer to it as an isolated entity. Thus was the idea of morality as a principle born. 69 Similar examples of the spreading process of abstraction can be found in Greek historical writing, in drama, the funeral oration of Pericles and other places. 70

THE SYMBOLIC INDUCEMENT OF LINGUISTIC FIXING

In our examination of the influences of writing on cognitive activity, we get a good look at the process of linguistic fixing and at the way symbolic inducement works in the symbol system of written language. First, the human mind-brain is naturally active, always engaged in creating and shaping meaning and constrained to stabilize experience so that it can somehow be dealt with. But with the advantages of written language the brain is freed from the burdens of memory and enabled to undertake cognitive processing at a new level. The instrument which provides the freedom, written language, is itself a product of mind-brain and naturally reflects, in principle, systematic cognitive operations. Written language is one more means of stabilizing experience which, at the instant of fixing, further encourages and sharpens stabilizing activities in certain ways. Writing induces reflexivity, and it can be perused in leisurely fashion and at a distance, so one's own ideas can be experienced in ways not possible without writing. Through its stabilizing action, writing encourages notions of stability and permanence and universality. It is itself an abstraction resulting from the mind's ability to abstract, and it further enhances and amplifies the lures of abstraction. It aids in the discovery and formulation of structure and pattern, but at the same time written language is open ended and flexible so that it serves and enhances certain aspects of creativity in the mind. Both written and spoken language share the potential to open and close experience in one operation; this is a reflection of the essential principle of ambiguity that is a part of all human perceptual activity. At the same time it is a rich means of expressing and sharing meaning, at once a bounding and explanatory system. Language, whether spoken or written, encourages identification and division at a single stroke.

All of these tendencies of mind-brain, sharpened and amplified in language and further stabilized in writing, inform manifestations of the Greek agonistic spirit. Greek fascination with the power of the word goes far back into prehistory. In the oral culture, the poet and the seer were essential repositories of cultural knowledge. They were believed to be the beneficiaries of a divine grace, receiving from the Muses the power of true speech.[71] This worshipful attitude toward the word came down to the Sophists, some of whom identified poetry with sacred magic. That idea is reflected in some of the writings of Gorgias, though a transformation was underway. By Gorgias' time the Greeks were trying to free themselves from what they perceived to be madness and irrationality, emotional forces beyond their control and capable of possessing them from time to time. Gorgias tried to emulate the magical powers of poetry through the technical manipulation of language.[72] In so doing, he sought to wed some uses of words with what would later be known as the "processes of rationality."

LANGUAGE AND RATIONALITY

The groundwork was laid for the development of the modes of rationality in the conditions of oral culture. Argument and disputation concerning pre-philosophical and pre-scientific matters evolved. Well before Aristotle, certain principles of disputation began to develop, later to be molded by Aristotle and others into a systematic logic. Anaximander may have been the first to argue on the basis of what came to be known as the principle of sufficient cause. Parmenides displayed argumentative method when he built structures of linked arguments from a secured starting point. Equally important, he appears to have been the first to set up an opposition between the senses and argument based on reason, and to opt for the latter. It was not empiricism that would be the mark of Greek thought but faith in reason. Parmenides, Zeno, and Melissus left evidence which allows them to be proclaimed "the first considerable exponents of rigorous deductive argumentation."[73]

The political climate of Greece encouraged direct attention to argument when the ability to persuade became an important value in the courts of law and in political forums. Lysias, Isocrates, Isaeus, Aeschines, and Demosthenes are a few who exhibited conscious concern about modes of argument in the fifth and early fourth centuries, B.C. Elsewhere a great deal of the argument centered upon medical matters. In general a premium was placed on the ability to demonstrate knowledge, but in mathematics the clearest conceptions of the formal conditions for proof show up. 74

All of these forces were pressures for systematizing procedures by which to discover what could be known and with what degree of certainty. The urge to create modes of discovery and demonstration led further to systematic creation of modes of dialectic and rhetoric. Arguments came to be designated as either necessary or probable, valid or invalid. Such concepts as "proof," "axiom," "hypothesis," "self-contradiction" and "consistency" were invented and defined.

These developments, which we might refer to as habits of mind, were spurred by the fact that tendencies toward them could be made enduringly explicit in writing, fixed for perception, and used in argument so that talk would further fix the gains of perception. It was not that the principles of logic, or the "laws of thought," were created by this process; rather, they came to be recognized explicitly. As Lloyd says, "It is not the case that the logic itself is *modified* by being made explicit, *except insofar as it is made explicit.*" He continues:

> In the instances we have taken we may speak of an increase in clarity, in explicitness and in self-consciousness: there is corresponding increase in confidence in the handling of certain types of argument in certain contexts. . . . But the formalization of logic consists—at least initially—in making explicit rules that are already contained in language and that are presupposed by intelligibility in communication. . . . The developments we have been dealing with involve a change in the level of awareness of aspects of reasoning. . . . 75

We do Lloyd no damage, I believe, if we interpret his use of the term "intelligibility," to mean principles of experiencing and meaning that are fundamental in certain aspects of symbolic processing and that are grounded in the cognitive and neurophysiological activity of mind-brain. The principles that we call collectively "intelligibility" function to induce "knowing," "feeling," and "doing."

What we must observe is that in their systematizing of rhetoric, the Greeks of the classical era chose to fix the principles of symbolic inducement in a particular way. They were lured symbolically by the promise of certain and permanent knowledge. This promise they perceived in the apparent precision and permanence of writing. It was no accident that for some, mathematics provided the model for all human thought. Mathematics seemed the most precise and enduring form of recordable thought. Insofar as it was a pursuit of the precise and the enduring, the

Greek Enlightenment is a magnificent celebration of human symbolic capacity. But only a portion of it. It was a turning away from "passion," "emotion," "imprecision," "ambiguity," "madness," in order to achieve better control of human destiny. Underlying it, one can glimpse what is surely one of the most profound of human emotions, namely, the desire to defeat time and gain immortality. And we can also see in the Greek position the tendencies that would lead us in the directions of the mind-body dichotomy, of equating meaning with language, and of belief that all knowledge is thoroughly and simply conscious social knowledge which can be made explicit.

THE NATURE OF LANGUAGE AS SYMBOL SYSTEM

We are now in a position to draw some general conclusions concerning the rhetoric of language as a symbol system. We can do so by considering what we have learned about the factors of symbolic inducement that are present when humans engage in language-centered contexts. Unless otherwise specified our conclusions apply both to written and spoken language.

1. *Whatever "meaning" and/or "knowing" is, it cannot be simply equated with, nor is it confined within, language.*

The support for this conclusion comes from several dimensions of human behavior. First, there is the recognition, several times supported in earlier sections of this book, that we know more than we can exhibit and we experience more than we can articulate. There can be no doubt that a tacit dimension of knowing exists, and that it is crucial to human intellectual development even though that knowledge eludes verbal articulation. For instance, there are avoidance behaviors and perceptual behaviors that we are prepared to perform from birth, without having to learn them. Moreover, in the development of a child, certain mathematical and logical laws and manipulations suddenly emerge and become operative without need for prior exposure or teaching. Language acquisition itself, as demonstrated by Piaget and Chomsky, is achieved with such speed and efficiency at certain developmental points that mimetic behavior and social learning could not possibly be wholly responsible. Furthermore, infants display intellectual activity and achievement prior to the development of language behavior. The arguments and evidence presented in previous sections of this book support the view that abstract processes in the brain operate to initiate mind-brain activity in such ways that some orders of "knowing" are present prior to environmental and social interaction. This is not to say that environment and interaction are not necessary to full psychological and intellectual development; it is simply to say that environment and social interaction are by no means sufficient to explain "meaning" and "knowing." In recent years the modes of study falling under the rubric of structuralism, which have replaced positivism and behaviorism, take into account the presence of knowledge that occurs without learning. In so doing scholarship adopts an outlook that more closely comports with the working of the mind-brain.

Language does not account for, nor correlate with, all that we perceive, experience, or feel. Everyone has had occasions when linguistic expression was inadequate to express all of the meaning and feeling occurring within himself or herself. Hence, a second dimension of behavior that argues against equating meaning with language is the inescapable personal and private stress on emphasis, value, and emotion that suffuses meaning. There are socio-cultural themes capable of evoking congruous meanings in large numbers of persons, but whatever meanings those themes have are the results of individual experiential transformations that reach well beyond the thematic language. There are always personal valences of meaning that lie below or above the surface of personal interaction and bear upon any meaning whatsoever. I previously quoted George Steiner on this matter. Let Steiner summarize the point here.

> Each living person draws, deliberately or in immediate habit, on two sources of linguistic supply: the current vulgate corresponding to his level of literacy, and a private thesaurus. The latter is inextricably a part of his subconscious, of his memories so far as they may be verbalized, and of the singular, irreducibly specific ensemble of his somatic and psychological identity. Part of the answer to the notorious logical conundrum as to whether or not there can be "private language" is that aspects of every language-act are unique and individual. They form what linguists call an "idiolect." Each communicatory gesture has a private residue. The "personal lexicon" in every one of us inevitably qualifies the definitions, connotations, semantic moves current in public discourse. The concept of a normal or standard idiom is a statistically-based fiction. . . . The language of a community, however uniform its social contour, is an inexhaustibly multiple aggregate of speech atoms, of finally irreducible personal meanings. 76

Because we know things we cannot express, knowledge and meaning are not confined by the limits of language. Because we have meanings that cannot be known by another, language only evokes partial understandings in others. None of this denies the special role that language has played in the development of our experiencing. But language and experiencing, though interactive and mutually constraining, are not the same.

2. *It is not correct to say that language creates thought, or that it mediates thought. Rather, language helps fix or stabilize tendencies and processes already present in thought and experience. In so doing it induces, both through its stabilizing function and through its own nature as a fixitive system.*

To say that language "creates" or "mediates" thought is to speak too baldly and too elegantly to be accurate. In the first place, neither language nor any other symbol system creates *ex nihilo*. Every symbol system must work with the materials of, and within the confines of, the cognitive processes of mind-brain. All symbolic manifestations result from processes initiated, indeed commanded by, higher cortical activity. This does not mean that language cannot be among the forces inducing us to perceive and experience in certain ways, nor does it mean that language plays no role in leading us to new insights. The flexibility of language allows us to combine words and phrases in myriad ways—indeed this is the rich resource poetry draws upon. The inventive power of metaphor is possible because the construction brings meaning contexts together so that a transformation occurs. One way to think of metaphoric action is to conceive of it as the transformational fixing of several apparently disparate meaning contexts. But language alone does not do the job. What so often defies articulation is the cognitive activity that seized upon the heretofore unnoticed similarity of structure or pattern in the first place. Whatever that activity is in full detail, it is a powerful and compressed example of the comparing, contrasting, and associating processes of mind-brain that are at the heart of "knowing." What metaphor offers is an instance of the linguistic fixing that stabilizes the cognitive action that is the shaper of meaning. Neither in this instance nor any other does language create meaning; language is one of the means, and probably the most flexible one, by which we stabilize meaning contexts.

The difficulty with the notion that language is a mediator of thought or meaning is that it too easily allows us to attribute both more and less power to language than we should. Words do not shape or channel meaning, they stabilize meaning that is within us. The meaning stabilized does not correspond on a one-to-one basis with words or patterns of words, but the stabilized meaning consists of structures that resonate within larger contexts existing in mind-brain. These contexts have cognitive histories that constitute important parts of their meanings. The contexts embody not just information, as we typically use that term, but valences that imbue the information with significance or lack of it, with degrees of relevance, with qualities of relationship to us. The contexts also include acts of judgment, states of feeling, veins of emotion. They tap tacit dimensions of cognitive activity. Indeed, within such a fulsome network "information" may constitute only a small portion of the total meaning structure. Finally, meaning contexts will include both conventional and idiosyncratic elements. In these ways meaning is always larger than language and is not easily contained by it as a bushel confines light or a mold restricts the flow of liquid.

At the same time, thought and language are very closely linked, for language behavior follows and partakes of the principles of thought. As we saw earlier, mind-brain is constantly engaged in the business of integrating experiences perceived from the environment with experiences internal to the neurophysiological and cognitive system of the human organism. The integrating processes are ongoing, never ending, and open-ended. Yet a constant part of these processes is the action of stabilizing experience so that it can be managed and used. Each of the senses has its modes of fixing, and these modes are complementary. Mind-brain is in charge of these fixing activities, but it adds further stabilizing dimensions of its own. The actions of bordering or structuring boundaries, of grouping and categorizing, of associating and relating, of concretizing and abstracting, and of creating hierarchical systems of nested meaning all function to achieve stabilization of meaning. Language, itself a stabilizing system, enhances, encourages, and in many instances completes the stabilizing proclivities of mind-brain. For example, language can further stabilize the gains of the sensory systems and present them, in integrated fashion, for expression, reflection, and communication. All of this is possible because language is a creature of those principles of mind-brain that induce and structure the stabilizing of experience. And at the same time, by its very nature language further induces the activity of fixing by offering the gains achieved or promised in the outcomes of fixing. There is a dual and reciprocal interaction here; the gains of one tendency are reinforced by the gains of the other. In this fashion the generally conservative development of meaning advances.

A striking feature of syntax provides a capping instance of the more-than mediative functions of language. Our verbal grammar provides syntactic structures that allow us to treat time in past, present, and future terms. Undoubtedly the remarkable discrimination that makes possible these syntactic distinctions is fundamental to human survival and a fundamental feature of cognitive functioning. It is not simply language that allows us to discriminate among times. It is an inherent capacity of mind-brain to "recollect" previously stabilized experience and to use it to plan ahead, to explore future possibilities, to be sustained and enriched by hopes, and to prepare cognitive defenses against contingencies not yet realized. Yet the structuring features of language that are the products of time discrimination and its uses can in turn direct those discriminations and uses. Language does not alone create our time oriented thoughts nor does it merely mediate time discriminations, but it does fix, fortify, and thereby direct time oriented thought—often in ways that significantly shape our personal and social natures:

> The language fabric we inhabit, the conventions of forwardness so deeply entrenched in our syntax, make for a constant, sometimes involuntary, resilience. Drown as we may, the idiom of time, so immediate to the mind, thrusts us to the surface. If this was not the case, if our system of tenses was more fragile, more esoteric, and philosophically suspect at its open end, we might not endure. Through shared habits of articulate futurity the individual forgets, literally "overlooks," the certainty and absoluteness of his own extinction. Through his constant use of tense-logic and time-scale beyond that of personal being, private man identifies, however abstractly, with the survival of his species.77

3. *Language encourages tendencies which are counterfactual.*

This conclusion deserves emphasis because of the narrow perspective often adopted in discussions of language and meaning. Discussion focuses on the "true" and "positive" aspects of language to the exclusion of its other aspects.

The problem at issue is analogous to problems we have in discussing reason. Until recently, a restricted view of reason prevailed. There existed an oppressive concern with notions of consistency and entailment, with verification and probity, with truth seeking and truth finding. These concerns focused more on models of behavior thought to be ideal than on actual behavior. Thinking so focused did not so much fail to recognize that human behavior refused to conform to the models as it tried to subordinate or stamp out those "aberrant" tendencies by exalting the "positive" and cloaking what did not fit the models in beggars' rags. Consistency was better than inconsistency; the logical was preferred over the illogical or the non-logical. By such practice, understanding of the meanings of these concepts was itself restricted, of course.

The same attitude carried over into discussions of communication behavior. In the latter half of the 1960s when rhetorical behaviors became vindictive and divisive, many critics eulogized "reason, civility, and decorum" and treated communication as if its only purposes were to be constructive, to achieve openness, to produce cooperation, commonality. Events and realities forced some degree of change among critics and commentators. Social protests aimed at securing rights for blacks, women, and others plainly had spokespersons who intentionally emphasized the positive functions of division and verbal attack. These were "facts" about practical communication that could not easily be denied, though in many discussions of communication theory and practice such "facts" continue to be neglected or are treated with distaste.

We see comparable attitudes in conventional treatments of language and meaning. Ambiguity is acknowledged, but clarity is preferred. Deceit is recognized as a fact of life, but veracity is lauded. The objective is to be sought and the distorted or subjective avoided. From time to time these powerful attitudes of preference lead commentators to hold certain language behaviors up for public display in order to deplore their probative wantonness and to engage in other purgative processes.

In all of these patterns of thought, where preference tends to hide or demean significant features of reality, the conventional perspective is shortsighted, missing powerful resources and enticements of both language and meaning. Language encourages the natural cognitive tendency to contemplate the future. This is surely an act that incorporates faith and hypothesis and illusion. And language has power to stabilize other flights of imagination as well. The human tendency to search for alternity can be seen in such linguistic phenomena as the verb form "to be," in the subject-predicate sentence, in the stating of general propositions, in terms that stand for abstract concepts, and in those verb forms that refer to past and future.

Language systems contain terms of negation as well as terms of affirmation. Consequently, we can deny what is and wish for something that is not.[78] The compulsion to say what is not, to posit otherness or alternity, says Steiner, is central to the mind and therefore to language. "We literally carry inside us, in the organized spaces and involutions of the brain, worlds other than the world. . . ."[79] Lying, he points out, is not mere miscorrespondence with fact; it is an active, creative agent. "The human capacity to utter falsehood, to lie, to negate what is the case, stands at the heart of speech and of the reciprocities between words and the world."[80] Truth and factuality do not count for the preponderance of typical speech behaviors, yet scholars of language and logic, reason and rhetoric, so often overlook this obvious state of affairs. But the resources of ambiguity, polysemy, fabrication, and denial are not pathologies; they are functional, productive, and, says Steiner, at the root of the genius of language.

> It is unlikely that man, as we know him, would have survived without the fictive, counter-factual, anti-determinist means of language, without the semantic capacity, generated and stored in the "superfluous" zones of the cortex, to conceive of, to articulate possibilities beyond the treadmill

of organic decay and death. It is in this respect that human tongues, with their conspicuous consumption of subjunctive, future and optative forms are a decisive evolutionary advantage. Through them we proceed in a substantive illusion of freedom. 81

Language refers to our internal states of experiencing and need to maintain cognitive balance as well as to matters that are outside of ourselves. This simply reflects the fact that our experiencing is internally directed and creative rather than being slavishly responsive to our physical environment. Our understanding of the inducements of meaning and language must be comprehensive enough to include the "fanciful" along with the "factual."

What, then, of language and symbolic inducement? Language is a product of mind-brain, therefore it should not be surprising to find that it follows the principles of cognition discussed in the second chapter of this book. Corresponding as it must to human experiencing, no formal model can ever adequately describe a system of language. We can say some things about how it functions, however. By its very nature as system, language provides a means of fixing experience, and at the same time it further induces the principles of fixing. Language interacts with cognition, further stabilizing cognitive processes. Its stabilizing actions are not confined to processes we have typically labeled "reasonable" or "rational," but they also lend encouragement to projection beyond what is, to fantasy and illusion and denial. These are phenomena that deserve more positive attention, especially in rhetorical study. Finally, I join others in insisting that language does not exist primarily to perform communicative functions. It exists as a rich and flexible means of "cutting the edges of experiencing." One of its significant by-products, however, is the means it gives us to enhance communing, communication, and social interaction. Social interaction thus becomes the third arena we must turn to in our examination of the principles of symbolic inducement.

NOTES

1. Midgely, 215.
2. For an account of these and other linguistic behaviors of chimps, see Eugene Linden, *Apes, Men and Language* (New York: Saturday Review Press, 1974).
3. Seymour Itzkoff, *Ernst Cassirer, Scientific Knowledge and the Concept of Man* (Notre Dame: University of Notre Dame Press, 1971), 194.
4. Midgley, 250.

5. Clifford Geertz, *the Interpretation of Cultures* (New York: Basic Books, 1973), 67.

6. Eric A. Havelock, *Prologue to Greek Literacy* (Cincinnati: University of Cincinnati Press, 1971), 19–21.

7. Ibid., 21.

8. Harry J. Jerison, "Paleoneurology and the Evolution of Mind," *Scientific American*, 234 (January 1976), 90–101.

9. Ibid., 101.

10. Ibid.

11. Havelock, *Origins of Western Literacy* (Ontario: The Ontario Institute for Studies in Education, 1976), 12.

12. Ibid., 10–11.

13. Steiner, 472.

14. Dennis Tedlock, "Toward an Oral Poetics," *New Literary History*, 8 (Spring 1977), 509.

15. O. H. Mowrer, "The Psychologist Looks at Language," *American Psychologist*, 9 (1954), 660–94.

16. C. E. Osgood, G. J. Succi, and P. H. Tannenbaum, *The Measurement of Meaning* (Urbana: University of Illinois Press, 1957).

17. J. J. Katz and J. A. Fodor, "The Structure of a Semantic Theory," *Language*, 39 (1963), 170–210. For a more complete development of the position, see J. J. Katz, *Semantic Theory* (New York: Harper & Row, 1972).

18. J. S. Sachs, "Recognition Memory for Syntactic and Semantic Aspects of Connected Discourse," *Perception and Psychophysics*, 2 (1967), 437–42.

19. S. Fillenbaum, "Memory for Gist: Some Relevant Variables," *Language and Speech*, 9 (1966), 217–27.

20. T. S. Hyde and J. J. Jenkins, "Recall of Words as a Function of Semantic, Graphic, and Syntactic Ordering Tasks," *Journal of Verbal Learning and Verbal Behavior*, 12 (1974), 471–80.

21. L. J. Rips, E. J. Shoben, and E. E. Smith, "Semantic Distance and the Verification of Semantic Relations," *Journal of Verbal Learning and Verbal Behavior*, 12 (1973), 1–20.

22. F. C. Bartlett, *Remembering: A Study in Experimental and Social Psychology* (Cambridge: Cambridge University Press, 1932), 213.

23. J. D. Bransford and J. J. Franks, "The Abstraction of Linguistic Ideas," *Cognitive Psychology*, 2 (1971), 331–50.

24. J. D. Bransford, J. R. Barclay, and J. J. Franks, "Sentence Memory: A Constructive versus Interpretative Approach," *Cognitive Psychology*, 3 (1972) 193–209.

25. For a more complete discussion of the findings of these studies, see J. D. Bransford and N. S. McCarrell, "A Sketch of a Cognitive Approach to Comprehension: Some Thoughts about Understanding What It Means to Comprehend," W. B. Weimer and D. S. Palermo, eds., *Cognition and the Symbolic Processes* (Hillsdale, N.J.: Lawrence Erlbaum Associations, 1974), 231–62.

26. Steiner, 414.

27. W. F. Brewer, "The Problem of Meaning and Higher Mental Processes" in Weimer and Palermo, eds., *Cognition and the Symbolic Processes*, 271.

28. Charles E. Osgood, William H. May, and Murray S. Miron, *Cross-Cultural Universals of Affective Meaning* (Urbana: University of Illinois Press, 1975).

29. Steiner, 212.

30. R. W. Brown and E. H. Lenneberg, "A Study in Language and Cognition," *Journal of Abnormal Social Psychology*, 59 (1954), 452–62.

31. Roger W. Brown, "Language and Categories," Appendix in Jerome S. Bruner, Jacqueline J. Goodnow, and George A. Austin, *A Study of Thinking* (New York: John Wiley and Sons, 1956), 247–310.

32. Gibson, *The Senses Considered as Perceptual Systems*, 282.

33. Havelock, "The Alphabetization of Homer," in Eric A. Havelock and Jackson P. Hershbell, eds., *Communication Arts in the Ancient World* (New York: Hastings House, 1978), 17.

34. Lentz, "The Oral Tradition of Interpretation: reading in Hellenic Greece as Described by Ancient Authors," 239–240.

35. Alexander Marshack, *The Roots of Civilization* (New York: McGraw-Hill, 1972), 117.

36. Ibid., 276–77.

37. Cassirer, *the Philosophy of Symbolic Form: Mythical Thought*, 23.

38. Ibid., 179.

39. Ibid., 54.

40. Ibid., 44–47.

41. Ibid., 40–50.

42. Ibid., 25.

43. Ibid., 98.

44. Havelock, *The Greek Concept of Justice* (Cambridge: Harvard University Press, 1978), 337.

45. Ibid., 180.

46. Ibid., 183.

47. Ibid., 42.

48. Ibid., 42–43.

49. Milman Parry, "Studies in the Epic Technique of Oral Verse-Making, I. Homer and Homeric Style," *Harvard Studies in Classical Philology*, 51 (1930), 80.

50. Havelock, *The Greek Concept of Justice*, 26.

51. Ibid., 38–41.

52. Kevin Robb, "Poetic Sources of the Greek Alphabet: Rhythm and Abecedarium from Phoenician to Greek," in *Communication Arts in the Ancient World*, 30.

53. Alfred Lord, *The Singer of Tales* (New York: Atheneum, 1976), 92.

54. Havelock, *Preface to Plato* (Cambridge: Harvard University Press, 1963), 127. © Harvard University Press 1963. Reprinted by permission.

55. See L. H. Jeffrey, *The Local Scripts of Archaic Greece* (Oxford: Oxford University Press, 1961).

56. Havelock, *Origins of Western Literacy*, 42–43.

57. Ibid., 49.

58. Havelock, *The Greek Concept of Justice*, 224.

59. Jack Goody, *The Domestication of the Savage Mind* (Cambridge: Cambridge University Press, 1977), 81.

60. Jack Goody and Ian Watt, "The Consequences of Literacy," *Comparative Studies in Society and History*, 5 (1963), 330.

61. Lloyd, 160.

62. Ibid., 299.

63. *Phaedrus*, 265 and 266, Edith Hamilton and Huntington Cairns, eds., *Plato: The Collected Works* (New York: Bollingen Foundation, 1961).

64. *Prior Analytics* 91b *et passim*, Richard McKeon, ed., *Introduction to Aristotle* (New York: Random House, 1947).

65. Ibid., 435.

66. Havelock, *Preface to Plato*, 298.

67. Havelock, *The Greek Concept of Justice*, 180–84.

68. Ibid., 221.

69. Ibid., 68.

70. See, for example, Friedrich Solmsen, *Intellectual Experiments of the Greek Enlightenment* (Princeton: Princeton University Press, 1975), 83–125.

71. Dodds, 81.

72. For a discussion of this matter see Jacqueline de Romilly, *Magic and Rhetoric in Ancient Greece* (Cambridge: Harvard University Press, 1975), esp. pp. 3–22.

73. Lloyd, *Magic, Reason and Experience*, 78.

74. Ibid., 103–23.

75. Ibid., 124.

76. Steiner, 46.

77. Ibid., 159–60.

78. Ibid., 221.

79. Ibid., 223.

80. Ibid., 214.

81. Ibid., 227.

4

SYMBOLIC INDUCEMENT AND
SOCIAL INTERACTION

In Chapter 3, I contended that language systems are symbolic manifestations of our cognitive capacities. While language interacts with perception and encourages perceptual patterns through stabilizing and fixing them, there is no strong evidence that language is the most important determinant of perception. The concept that best helps us understand the perception-language-meaning relationship is the closed feedback loop, with the interaction of all points on the loop being mutually dependent and mutually interactive.

Similarly, closed feedback loop activity best explains the interaction between cognitive processing and social behavior. Humans are, of course, social and cultural beings. But we should not let that truism blind us. Because there are always observable manifestations of social behaviors, it becomes tempting to equate the most important dimensions of meaning with the apparent norms, rules, and structures of social activity. One can even find the human brain referred to as a uniquely social brain. Uniqueness is wrongly assigned here, for animals, birds, and insects have societies that are as important in their ways as our society is to us. It is sometimes alleged that we are products of our environments. It is the case that a significant portion of the human forebrain awaits development following birth. But it is a serious mistake to assume that social contexts are so constraining that our cognitive processes can be socially determined in such important ways that to manipulate the contexts will necessarily assure modifications in cognitive processes. As Midgley observes, society is no alternative to genetic programming. Society requires genetic programming, and the more complicated and sophisticated the society, the richer the programming must be. "When we try to study human society without reference to that programming, we are abstracting from a species repertoire that we take for granted."1 Sociobiologist Edward Wilson has compiled a book full of evidence that undermines the "misconception among many of the more traditional Marxists, some learning theorists, and a still surprising proportion of anthropologists and sociologists that social behavior can be shaped in virtually any form."2 While there are reasons to question some of Wilson's specific claims, it is impossible to deny his major conclusion without ignoring a substantial amount of contradictory evidence.

At the same time, we are equally mistaken to attribute human symbolic behavior simply to genetic programming. The fact that the forebrain re-

95

mains to be developed after birth means that environmental factors, heavily laced with socio-cultural aspects, are essential to its development. As Geertz points out, a kind of gap exists between neurophysiological tendencies and potentialities and the ultimate manifestations they may assume. What was said about language in Chapter 3 shows that we are not tightly wired mechanisms responding to absolutely determined and controlled programs. For this reason, says Geertz, the human is "the animal most desperately dependent upon such extragenetic, outside-the-skin control mechanisms, as cultural programs for ordering his behavior."3

In his discussion of the development of social behavior Lenneberg has provided the perspective for exploration to follow. He notes that at various key developmental points, an organism becomes maturationally ready to respond to and to interact with specific forms of external stimulation. Such stimulation is then essential for further, healthy development. But while it is correct to say that the stimulation in question is essential, it is not correct to assume that that stimulation is necessarily the cause that shapes the development. It is better to conceive of the interaction between organism and stimulation as one in which the organism is ready to "resonate" with a particular pattern of stimulation and, upon exposure, will begin so to resonate. In this sense and to this degree we are right to conclude that "impoverished social input may entail permanently impoverished behavior patterns."4 However, the resonating activity of the organism will be constrained by principles of cognitive activity already operative in the organism and, of course, those principles are prone to modification, extension, and transformation as results of the resonating process. It is necessary to remember, too, that humans do not have separate categories of activity; for example, they do not have mental activity as opposed to social activity. Furthermore, humans undergo continuing interaction with the shaping and inducing principles of symbolic action pervasive all along the way. We cannot justly think of *a* stimulus engendering or impeding social development:

> In the case of the individual and society we need to learn ways of thinking and feeling which will enable us genuinely to know each in the other's terms, which is as near as we can ordinarily get to saying that we are studying forms of organization in a continuous process: the brain, the nervous system, the body, the family, the group, the society, man. There is no real point at which we can break off this process, to isolate an independent substance. Yet equally we cannot select any one of them and make the others dependent on it. If the old individualism artificially isolated the "bare human being," there is equal danger in certain trends in the new sociology which isolate the group, the society or the culture as an absolute point of reference. 5

If we ask what social stimulation is as experience, the answer must be: Socio-cultural interaction has meaning and stabilizes experience in accord with the principles of cognition that are initiated by mind-brain. The process of social fixing entails more than an action which stabilizes; social fixing also serves to reinforce, encourage, enhance, magnify, extend, and transform tendencies inherent in the nature of cognitive function. All such activity is stirred by a mobilized search for external phenomena with which to resonate so that the processes of cognitive activity may be further developed and fulfilled.

We do not have simple neurological determinism to account for human behavior, nor do we have simple environmental or cultural shaping. We have, always, a mixture of the two, one dependent upon the other. Our neurological capacity makes all of our experiencing possible, and it is not freewheeling, but is constrained by certain principles of operation. At the same time, neurological capacities must develop through interacting with external phenomena to achieve their full sophistication. Human culture is a reflection of the functioning of the human brain, and simultaneously, the brain acts upon, responds to, and constantly monitors its own state in light of the constraints of culture already in place.

In Chapter 2 on mind-brain I pointed out that one of the difficulties of writing a description of mind-brain activity is that linguistic narrative must have a beginning and an ending, and in writing, especially, other forms must move in a linear fashion. Thus the ongoing, interactive nature of cognitive activity becomes distorted linguistically as one momentarily fixes such activity in order to express some abstract understanding of it. The same difficulty faces us in dealing with symbolic inducement and social interaction. Mind-brain is busily resonating prior to birth, acting upon, interacting with, and accommodating to materials presented by an external environment. The action is continuous, multifaceted, and interlocking, and such action continues and becomes more complex after birth. Despite the enforced peculiarities of written language that mark the pages ahead, the dynamic interplay of forces and influences needs to be recalled constantly as discussion proceeds.

It must also be remembered that no formal or closed model can give an account of the functions of cognition except in principle. The flexibility of cognitive functioning is the reason; it generates ever present possibilities for multidirectional change. The possible manifestations of cognition are too numerous and too rich to accommodate comprehensive explanation, perhaps in conception and certainly in prose or graphic representation. Accordingly, the manifestations of language as symbol system defy exhaustive description, for language operates on the principles of cognition.

It should surprise no one, then, that the discussion that follows does not account for the full panoply of socio-cultural interactions experienced by humans, or for all the characteristics of symbolic inducement that are features of those interactions. I shall, however, try to deal with the principles of symbolic, social inducement and suggest some of the directions they may take in their development.

Where can an examination of symbolic inducement and social interaction conveniently and clarifyingly begin? My interest is in fundamentals; therefore it seems logical to begin with behaviors at infancy. Here there are some fairly convincing data, basic principles of behavior are established, but complexity is not yet overwhelming. By the time they are adults, individuals enter social interactions with established personal and relational tendencies and patterns so varied that they can scarcely be traced. Facing such personal, group, and public histories in action, it could be extremely difficult to get at the roots of symbolic inducement. These are reasons to begin investigation of symbolic inducement and social interaction with consideration of the conditions of infancy.

Each of the systems of human sensory apparatus is operative at birth, though they exist in varying degrees of sophistication and it is difficult to know which is dominant. For example, consider the current practice of bonding the newborn with the mother immediately following birth. As the infant is held on the mother's stomach, is it touch or smell that plays the larger role in bonding? And what of audition? The baby will be treated to the cooings and gurglings and other murmurings of excitement that accompany emergence of new, infant life. That the infant's first impressions occur in combination is a reasonable conclusion to draw; the exact valences of the combinations will probably never be determined. But let us somewhat arbitrarily consider vision and audition as modes of experiencing social interaction in infancy. We noted earlier the interpenetration of comprehension and vision. Audition is a significant mode of experiencing the world because most of the infant's first contact with the social entreaties of language will occur via this sensory channel. And, of course, both vision and audition are obviously central avenues of social inducement. How, then, do these modes of becoming aware of the outside world operate in the experiences of a developing child?

VISUAL INTERACTION WITH THE WORLD IN INFANCY

Casual observation of newborn infants encourages the perception that nourishment and sleep constitute the be-all and end-all of existence in early development. In the period immediately following birth, an infant awakens at fairly regular intervals, seems primarily interested in assuaging

98

hunger, then rather quickly falls back to sleep. This pattern varies among infants, but generally speaking it describes rather well the ostensible behavior of the first few weeks. Actually, much more is going on in preparation for development.

The infant arrives, not only with a need to seek food for bodily growth, but with an innate tendency to search for cognitive stimulation. Certain predilections for perceptual and intellectual patterns are already operative. In normal children these predilections function to constrain cognitive activity so that the needed stimulation does not overwhelm the infant but is used productively. Any change in the level of sensory stimulation has the potential to be noticed by the infant both neurophysiologically and cognitively, and adjustive responses follow. For example, a reduction in the auditory level of a sound pattern will decrease the sensory stimulus being received, but the reduction can, in fact, increase cognitive stimulation as it offers the possibility of comparison of the changed acoustical stimulations.

The infant's visual system is not yet finely tuned, so visual focus is one of the important constraints—adults say "problems"—operating in the early months of life. It is significant for our purpose to realize that an infant focuses most sharply on objects about eight inches away from its face. This means the face of a mother or caregiver offers itself as a fairly constant candidate for the infant's perception. Further, there is general agreement that the design characteristics of the human face correspond with evolved, innate visual preferences of infants.[6] Thus, early visual experiencing, which provides material for cognitive activity, features a potent social component. For the first several months of life, the infant's attentiveness to such phenomena as facial displays will be determined largely by conventional patterns of child handling and by internal patterns or principles of excitation in the brain. In other words, the infant's attention will be caught and captivated for short periods of time by external events that interrupt and intrude upon the infant's consciousness. But by the third month, the infant will begin to exercise control over its attention, and so will start to direct and sustain perception.

What is the nature of the experiencing that an infant will begin to construct from its interactions with a caregiver's face? We cannot know for sure, of course; certainly we do not yet know all there is to know. But we can be confident that infants do not have well developed means for sharing experiences. Yet there is good reason to believe that states of feeling and emotion are at the core of infants' interactions. Students of child development have discovered that the combinations and constellations of facial movements and positions that display such emotions as fear, joy, anger, disgust, and surprise are largely innate. The physical displays that accompany such emotions tend to evoke mimetic and other responses from caregivers. Over time, such behaviors on the parts of caregiver and infant become interactive and mutually reinforcing. Satisfactions are gained by both parties involved in the symbolic exchange. Thus, the seeds of symbolic-social inducement are initially encouraged, nurtured, and consolidated through the mutual interplay of emotional displays on the part of caregiver and infant.7

Although the exact nature of all that is consolidated during early interplay with caregivers eludes us, the fundamental elements or principles of interaction are not too difficult to surmise. Somehow, the infant has to begin to comprehend ongoing interaction as "units" in order to transcend what could otherwise be continuously encountered as an always confusing flux of behavior and feeling. Visual sensory experience of perceiving facial characteristics will be aided by the mother or caregiver who constructs particular kinds of behavioral patterns that make it easier for the infant to induce the experience of unitary meaning. For instance, facial features peculiar to certain kinds of expression are typically exaggerated by the caregiver, so that an emphasizing of those features can be visually perceived. In addition, each individual facial expression tends to be bounded by units of relative passivity and silence; the cognitive principle of bordering or edging can therefore work in the interaction of caregiver and infant. The caregiver helps the infant cope with the problem of knowing where a unit begins and ends, and the infant's mind-brain is designed to follow such a principle of coping. Another strategy employed by caregivers is that of slowing their behavioral actions so that the internal mechanisms of the infant can more readily process what is being perceived. Slower paced behavior also encourages the infant to focus on features of behavior that are constant. Finally, caregivers typically repeat behaviors, creating what are called runs. This enhances the fixing of constancies in the infant's perceptual world. All of these particular strategies and more work together to induce structuring of boundaries and units, a kind of structuring for which the infant is genetically prepared by virtue of the cognitive principle of edging or bordering. The child is by nature a discriminator and in the instances I am discussing is prepared to "resonate" with stimulation offered.

There are several other principles at work in this sensory interaction. The repetitions of caregivers' behaviors that constitute runs will be composed of very similar, but not absolutely identical, behaviors. It is difficult to smile precisely the same way time after time. Consequently, what occurs in repetitive runs may be likened to the process of playing variations on a theme; a principle of constancy will be manifested across contiguous minor divergencies. Hence, the cognitive tendency to search for similarities and group them together and the accompanying tendency to respond to differences that matter will be encouraged. Cognitive capacities for both assimilation and differentiation are sharpened. Moreover, the roots of processes of abstraction that will flower throughout later cognitive development are nurtured.

The foregoing behavioral phenomena and symbolic principles combine to achieve the visual-sensory portion of the unit of interpersonal interaction. The central points here are that even in the relatively visual stimulation and experiencing we have been considering, the characteristics of the social stimulation invite "interpretation" on the basic principles of mind-brain activity and at the same time nurture and fortify those principles of processing—always symbolically—the data of social stimulation.

Similar resonance, contributing to the structuring of unitary experience, occurs in an infant's experiencing of motor activity. The infant's visual-sensory experience will be a function of motor activity to a large extent. During interaction with a caregiver the infant will not be passive but will be moving, making sounds, and providing visual displays. As a result of these activities the infant may view the caregiver straight on for a portion of time, then move its head so that the caregiver appears in peripheral vision. Even if the caregiver's behavior remains unchanged, the sensory-motor experiences of the infant will be considerably different. Still more complex alteration occurs if the caregiver's behavior changes following changes in behavior on the part of the infant. For instance, the infant may change facial expression, and then see the caregiver break into a smile in return. This kind of responsive interaction encourages the structuring of temporal units of contingent relationship. At least sometimes the infant perceives the muscular movement of its own behavior, the pause, and then the response of the caregiver. It could not happen if the infant were not innately equipped to create symbolic units out of flows of external events. Of course, the experiences will differ depending on whether the caregiver acts to encourge structuring of interactive experience by initiating behavior change at the exact time the infant does or chooses not to respond in any very noticeable way.

In the functions of motor activity in conjunction with sensory-visual experience there are also the roots of another cognitive principle that operates in association with those already mentioned. The bases of self/other discriminations are present. Repetition of motor activity by the infant may be accompanied by a variety of behaviors emanating from the caregiver. On the other hand, a variety of infant motor activities may exact relatively unchanging behavior on the part of the caregiver. To the extent that the infant discriminates between these different kinds of response and interaction, possibilities for self/other distinctions are established. Stern summarizes the point this way:

> On the one hand, I am pointing out the enormous extent to which the infant's sensory experience is determined by the nature of his motor experience, resulting in a fused experience. On the other hand, I am saying that to the extent that his sensory experience is not reliably determined by the nature of his motor experience, resulting in a multiplicity of sensori-motor experiences built around the same motor experience, to that extent he can begin to uncouple the self-other fusion. 8

The infant behaves in some outward fashion and perceives an outward behavior of the caregiver in response. But, behaving in the same fashion again may result in a somewhat different or a very different response on the part of the caregiver. The infant may begin to perceive that there is not a necessary, contiguous relationship between its own behavior and the behavior of the caregiver. There is the possibility in this kind of ongoing exchange for recognition that phenomena in the external environment are not merely extensions of the infant's behaviors. Such recognition is necessary for the development of concepts of "self" and "other."

A component of any unit of interpersonal experience will be experience of affective phenomena. Such affective phenomena can take the forms of feelings of excitation, of pleasure, of states of expectation, and so on. Or they may be experienced as boredom, loss of excitement, apprehension, or states of overexcitement or excessive stimulation. Here again, to exist as states, say, fear, not pleasure, feelings must be demarcated. Feelings of excitation and anticipation, or feelings of diminishing excitation or pleasure plainly call up different activities in infants. This can best be explained in terms of principles of bordering or edging—symbolic constructions of experience. My claims are that human infants innately discriminate even their states of feeling, and that affective experience further induces discrimination.

Sensory-visual, motor, and affective experiencings jointly constitute the interpersonal unit of experience. Interpersonal experience is not the sum of sensory, motor, and affective experience but their product. Infant/caregiver interaction is composed of multitudes of units of sensory-motor-affective interaction joined together over periods of time. The units, too, undergo structuration. Both parties to interaction begin to form linkages among the units and structure clusters which become synthesized into larger networks of meaning. As these networks become more comprehensive, and more stable and durable through repetition, an interactive history becomes established to influence subsequent interaction, and in turn to be modified by it. Patterns of interrelationship thus develop their own individual characteristics and directions, so that what may appear to be similar interactions among differing parties may actually have quite different outcomes that reflect different developing theories.

Early infant-caregiver interactions reveal the beginnings of the processes through which cognitive activities become manifest in social behaviors. The flow of interaction is symbolically structured into meaningful units through pauses and repetition. As behaviors are repeated and varied over time, infants are invited to compare and perceive similarities and differences. Because infants do not control the behavioral changes of the caregiver, infants are provided opportunities to begin to perceive self and other. Social interaction induces further social interaction, the inducements strengthened by affective states that accompany and result from behaviors. These operations are characteristic of all human social behavior.

AUDITORY INTERACTION IN INFANCY

A hypothesis offered by Dance is that an acoustic trigger for conceptualization is the most basic source of self/other realizations. By "acoustic trigger," Dance means an early and fundamental experience with sound that encourages an infant to perceive beyond itself. It seems to me both common sense and a good deal of data support Dance's hypothesis; therefore I shall examine the hypothesis and associated evidence in some detail. For our purposes, it is not important that one accept the idea that an acoustic trigger is the most fundamental experience that moves toward conceptual thought, though I believe the argument on its behalf is a strong one.

Just as the infant seems to be innately tuned to resonate visually to a human face, so infants appear to prefer resonating acoustically with the sound patterns of the human voice.[9] It is significant for Dance's hypothesis that the infant's acoustical sensory apparatus appears to be operative prior to birth, but the visual sensory apparatus does not become operative until birth, and an infant must develop for some three months before its visual acuity can compare with that of adults. Audition in young infants, on the other hand, is astonishing.[10] To illustrate that point let us consider briefly the nature of discrimination of speech sounds.

If one wanted to picture the acoustical, physical difference between a sound such as "ba" and another, "pa," the difference would have to be shown in terms of a finely discriminated continuum. Acoustically, there is no sharp break between the two sounds. The middle zone of our continuum would represent sounds so similar that a human listener could not detect whether these intermediate sounds fell toward the "ba" or the "pa"

103

ends of the continuum. However, in the last decade research has shown that humans do not perceive sounds as differing by continuous degrees. At a given point on the continuum, humans perceive abrupt change; at a specific point humans cease to perceive sounds as belonging to the "ba" end of the continuum and identify them as being on the "pa" end. We must conclude from this that consonant perception is categorical rather than continuous. It does not seem unreasonable to suppose that such categorical listening developed and sharpened in the human over time. One might think also that discernment of precise acoustic discontinuities would be beyond the capability of an infant. However, Eimas has demonstrated that that supposition is false; young infants perceive categorically the same ways as adults. 11 We must conclude, then, that the infant's acoustic sensory apparatus not only operates early but operates with a high degree of sophistication. Because sophisticated auditory abilities are already operating at birth, it is reasonable to assume they play a role in the early development of cognition.

The acoustic sensory system may be better able to induce realizations of the complementary experiencing of "me-ness" and "other-ness" than other sensory systems in infancy. The visual system, as Dance explains, is largely beyond the control of the infant. While it may close its eyes and turn its head, the infant has very little to do with the visual stimuli presented to it. Consequently, visual displays may be said to occur outside of or beyond the infant. On the other hand, the infant's tactile, kinesthetic, and proprioceptive experiences are primarily internal. The exception would occur when the infant was being handled, in which case the experience would be primarily external. 12 In either case, in early infancy, before motor development has come under the control of the child, these sensory experiences do not seem to present clear-cut opportunities for a combined "me-ness," "other-ness" experience.

An infant plays an active role in creation of its own sound; in other words, in production of its own acoustic stimuli. This is less true where other sensory systems operate. As Dance puts it, "With the utterance of sound, and the acoustic perception of sound, there is the beginning of a distinction, within the infant, between total subjectivity and the diminution of subjectivity."13 In the act of producing sound, the infant can perceive movements of the musculature that are engaged during vocal production; as a result of the act the infant can experience the sound that appears to occur outside of its own body. If the infant's attention moves from the internalized utterance as muscular action to the external sound as product, there will be at least some reduction in subjective self-sensing and a growth in awareness of objectivity and of perception of states existing outside of self. Most important, perhaps, is the possibility of experiencing a relationship between the two. The importance of such experiencing for comprehension and communication needs no elaboration. As Dance sees it, the most significant benefit for the infant's cognitive development is the realization of contrast. 14

As we have seen elsewhere in this book, discriminating borders are fundamental to cognitive activity. The recognition and conceptualization of contrast is fundamental to experiencing, to learning, and to meaning. Dance further points out the heuristic contribution of contrast conceptualization when he emphasizes that "decentering" and "displacement" are two features of sophisticated symbolic processing, encouraged by the acoustic trigger. As Dance uses the terms, decentering is the ability to recognize that there is a world beyond the self, that it is populated by other selves, and that one can try to consider the perspectives of others when determining one's own behavior. By displacement Dance refers to the ability to experience meaning outside of present time and place, to think about what was, to contemplate what might occur, to consider timeless matters. Central to our concerns is the fact that the acoustic sensory system can encourage both centering and displacement as symbolic processes, because audition features time in a way not matched in the other systems.

Whether or not they are the very first features of social interaction to trigger conceptualization, acoustic stimuli must rank high among the events of infancy that lead to sophisticated symbolic behavior. As we have seen, our systems of meaning are constructed on principles of contrast, explicitly and implicitly. The ambiguities and tensions that exist because of self-other relationships color all of our lives, and as Kenneth Burke indicates, those ambiguities offer the characteristic invitation to rhetorical behavior. 15 Contrast provides choice, and thus is an inducement to choice making or partisan behavior. To be aware of time, and simultaneously to possess the capacity to transcend time or deny time and construct alternity, encourages the possibilities of imagination, fancy, and illusion, phenomena not at all inimical to rhetorical behavior. Comprehension and symbolic inducement are joined together in everlasting partnership in these symbolic processes, of which auditory experience is especially and perhaps even primordially productive of opportunities and demands for discriminating and bounding time, self, other, distances, place, and other crucial cognitions.

AUDITORY RHYTHM

Before we leave the topic of vocal production, there are several other features of audition and vocalization that warrant attention. Let us return to infant/caregiver interaction to note the obvious fact that vocalic production will be a significant part of that kind of interaction. The mother or caregiver will engage in a great deal of sound-making behavior, and the infant will produce a variety of sounds just because it has the physical capacity to do so. Caregivers mimic the baby's sounds because they are cute, and continual interactions of sound production will constitute interpersonal runs even though control is unevenly exercised in the exchange. Stern points out that a caregiver's use of tempo, or rhythm, often operates to stimulate the arousal level of an infant. In fact, rhythm will not only be employed in vocalic production, in singing or chanting for example, but the caregiver often engages in clicking and clucking sounds, in the clapping of hands, and so on. These are all behaviors that engage and presumably encourage the infant's sense of tempo, rhythm, or timing.16

It appears that there is much more involved here than play. In his discussion of language, Lenneberg provides a detailed and technical explanation of the function of rhythm in language development. Rhythmic activity, he points out, is a fundamental property of the vertebrate brain. It is no surprise, then, to recognize that thought occurs temporally, and that matters of timing will be inextricably bound up with matters of comprehension and conceptualization. Naturally, rhythm is intimately involved in the development of speech. As Lenneberg explains, evidence shows that children do not begin to develop speech "until their brains have attained a certain degree of electro-physiological maturity, defined in terms of an increase with age in the frequency of the dominant rhythm. Only when this rhythm is about 7 cps or faster (at about age two) are they ready for speech development."17 Lenneberg points out further that rhythm appears to constitute the organizing principle for the recognition and comprehension of sound patterns. For these reasons, he concludes that in the human, "the rhythmic motor sub-serves a highly specialized activity, namely speech."18

The importance of rhythm may extend beyond enabling speech, because Berry finds that the primal modality of audition exercises a kind of tonic influence on the brain's entire activity. Audition operates to influence the level of activity and stability of the central nervous system. Berry suggests that if the spontaneous rhythm of the auditory system is impaired, the stability of other sensory and allied systems may suffer as well.19 There is support for this idea in the research of Condon, who used microkinesic sound film analysis to illustrate the timing or rhythmic disorder suffered by autistic and similarly dysfunctional children.20 Rhythm appears to be central to levels of arousal, to emotional states, to pattern recognition, and indeed to conception and comprehension. Rhythm underlies the processes of knowing, the behaviors of social interaction, and can induce symbolic involvement and action.

ARTICULATION, INTENTION, AND MEANING

There is not complete agreement on the matter, but a number of students of cognition and of speech and language behavior believe there is a close relationship between the ability to perceive spoken sounds in a meaningful way and use of articulatory mechanisms activated in the production of vocalic sound. Luria posits that in the early years development of speech in the child occurs through comparing the structures involved in the physical production of speech with the structures that embody the speech sound. [21] Turvey points to the evident "tight coupling" between such structures, suggesting that listeners are able to make sense of articulation because of the correspondence between the invariants of sound vibration and the invariants of articulation. [22] Halwes and Wire express the same idea when they refer to the "strict isomorphism between the linguistically relevant aspects of the acoustic signal, and the linguistically relevant aspects of the articulatory gestures, the former being produced directly by the latter." [23]

We do know that typically the sounds of speech are processed in the major or left cerebral hemisphere, while non-speech sounds are processed in the right hemisphere. There are differences of opinion over whether some kind of special auditory decoding process for speech sounds exists in the brain. If such a process did exist, it would seemingly have to involve a rather straightforward comparison of incoming speech sounds with a set of phonemic patterns stored in the brain. But there is no evidence to indicate this kind of comparison occurs; in fact, the evidence seems to indicate that it cannot occur. Consequently, the more likely explanation, offered by the scholars cited above, is that speech sounds are perceived in terms of processes involved in the production of those sounds. Liberman et al. summarize the position and suggest a most interesting common ground for experience:

> There is typically a lack of correspondence between acoustic cue and perceived phoneme, and in all these cases it appears that perception mirrors articulation more closely than sound. If this were not so, then, for a listener to hear the same phoneme in various environments, speakers would have to hold the acoustic signal constant, which would, in turn, require that they make drastic changes in articulation. Speakers need not do that—and in all probability cannot. . . . This supports the assumption that the listener uses the inconstant sound as a basis for finding his way back to the articulatory gestures that produced it and thence, as it were, to the speaker's intent. [24]

If this interpretation is correct, when we engage in communicative acts with others, we are involved in a comparison of our understanding of our own intentions with the presumed intentions of others. Only so could we comprehend sound patterns in meaningful ways. Undoubtedly a great deal of the comparative process would take place in the out-of-awareness or tacit dimensions of thought, though all levels of awareness could potentially be involved. Whether or not the interpretation is ultimately found to be accurate, it calls to our awareness the undoubted fact that interpretation of intentions is an activity inherent in symbolic inducement wherever language occurs. The visual sensory system, the auditory sensory system, supported by each of the other sensory systems, engage in the symbolic process of detecting and structuring contrasts, not just of sounds or graphic features but of the motives that could lead to their construction. By their nature contrasts produce the possibility of choice; they invite choice-making behavior. Choice making, in turn, induces intention and judgment of intentions. From the innate need to organize the environment and to structure meaning at one pole to the explicit attempt to motivate fellow humans to join a cause at the other pole, intentionality is ever-present in human behavior and an inevitable feature of inducement wherever symbols are processed.

The intellect of an infant is obviously active and resonating with the external environment before a single recognizable word has been spoken. The search for cognitive order has begun. Some believe that even during the first month of life, the infant starts to structure sensory-motor schemes for action. 25 In any case, there is no doubt that such schema are rapidly developed in the first four months of life. There is little doubt that during this time they come under the control of vision. Then, during the second four-month period, infants become interested in what effects their motor activity is having on the external environment, and the baby begins to explore objects. For the first time, the infant engages in behaviors that can be described as the beginning of social extroversion.

In these early months of life, infants will be resonating to vocalized sounds produced by various caregivers and will commence the babbling that is the precursor of language. What the babbling seems to reveal is that the child reacts to holistic sound patterns; the first discernible features of language the child will produce are intonation patterns resembling exclamations, questions, and so on. True to natural cognitive tendencies, what the infant seems first to react to and produce are sound patterns and structures. These may not yet be "language," but these early patterns will form the basis of language development. 26

In the newborn infant, then, we have cognitive processes not only prepared to interact with the environment, including other persons, but needing to do so in order to achieve maturity. With states of feeling and emotion at its base, infant cognition operates in accord with principles of contrast and bordering, searches for similarities and differences, responds to constancies, and begins to link behaviors and interactions into clusters of behaviors and interactions. The fundamentals of self-other object and self-other person distinctions become established early. The infant is encouraged to respond to sound patterns as meaning patterns and in turn to produce sound patterns. Equipped with fortified bordering capacities the baby begins to refine vocalic and auditory repertoires. There is strong reason to believe that intention operates at the core of auditory meaning patterns, providing a fundamental cognitive aid for understanding what the meanings are. The development of sensory motor schemes for behaving, cognitive models or maps if you will, indicates that the infant is motivated to know the external environment and to have an effect upon it. The world of the infant, then, is one in which responses to symbolic inducements are underway, and production of such inducements is encouraged.

THE DEVELOPMENT OF LANGUAGE

Our attention must now turn to language development, not because we are interested in it for its own sake, but because the features of language development correspond with certain cognitive developments that have fundamental roles in social behavior. We want to know what cognitive principles and processes of inducement undergo projection or transformation from structures of the mind to manifestation in the structures of social interaction.

To reiterate a point made in other ways earlier, the nature/nurture question with regard to both language development and social behavior is specious. It is thoroughly established that children develop language on a schedule so rapid and so precise that the developments cannot be accounted for in terms of social interaction. At the same time, there is no question but that stimulation from the external environment, including social interaction, is essential for the full maturation and realization of normal language capability. It seems fairly clear that at certain key points along the developmental path, a child's cognitive processes become ready to resonate with certain kinds of stimuli, and that the child will search out the needed stimuli in order to proceed. When such points are reached, remarkable leaps in language ability are demonstrated. What is happening is that the child is building the structures of linguistic fixing in accord with his or her developing processes of cognition. As Lenneberg puts it:

> Strictly speaking, words are not labels of fixed and conventionally agreed upon classes of objects but labels or modes of categorization; they characterize a productive, creative process, and the same is true of the

categorization of the deeper schemata called phrase-markers. If language functioned by agreement, instead of merely labeling types of processes, utterances would be extremely limited in scope, we could not talk about anything new, and it would take many more years for children to acquire a stock of *what* to say. 27

Roger Brown confirms Lenneberg's conclusion, but by using a different strain of evidence that bears directly on the role of social interaction in development of language. Brown notes that there is little evidence to support the notion that children improve their language skills in order to achieve accuracy and precision, or general clarity, in social interaction with others. However logical this sort of motivation might seem to an observer, Brown shows that available data indicate that young children show a marked lack of concern for making themselves clear. Put in perhaps a better way: they just assume they will be understood. 28 This does not signal steadily evolving social sensitivity, but sensitivity to the meanings and possibilities of social interaction probably develop with as much complexity and periodicity as acquisition of linguistic skills. In both cases the developmental leaps that occur rule out imitation or social agreement as the fundamental factors determining a young person's schedule of social learning. We can see this more clearly if we return to consideration of an infant's development.

The first months of life are marked by the infant's assimilation of the external world to its own body. 29 Those objects and persons that are perceived are perceptually centered within the infant's own activity and are simply seen to be on the same plane of existence. The child is at the center of its universe. During this period, the infant is so thoroughly ego-centered that it has no developed conceptualization of self because the full realization of others, both objects and persons, remains to be constructed. The seeds for such realization are already active, however, in the sensory systems. During the first two years, the infant will begin to develop notions of space and time, and, with the egocentric outlook still prevailing, primitive notions of causality will be constructed. During this period affective development occurs hand in hand with cognitive advances. The process here is holistic rather than differentiated, and evidences of emotion can be easily recognized. 30 An elemental manifestation of affect can be seen in the infant's visible demonstrations of fear at losing physiological equilibrium. Equilibrium is a state of being that is neurophysiologically and psychologically secure and comforting. Throughout all stages of cognitive development (and it is now agreed that such development continues beyond adolescence), human behavior can be described as the search for various states of equilibrium.

Suddenly, at about age two, the child begins language behavior. There appear to be two major consequences of this development. Inner states of feeling and experiencing become solidified, enhanced, and extended through the inducement of linguistic fixing. The inner world of the child will begin to become an object of contemplation in ways it had not been before. At the same time, rudimentary communication will encourage the kinds of response from others that will eventually lead to a recognition of and appreciation for the autonomous and permanent nature of others. At this stage, social perception is a highly general, superficial kind of experiencing. The child will perceive the overt behaviors of others in holistic ways; the subtle nuances which would indicate sarcasm, or irony, or forced gaiety, or restrained anger will tend to be missed. And because the child is largely ego-centered in terms of time and space, the past behaviors of others will not be efficiently used as guidelines for future action. 31 This is also the period when a nascent morality will begin to develop, as the child perceives and interacts with the authoritarian structure of adults. 32 The groundwork is now being established for a reduction of the totally egocentric world of pleasurable/uncomfortable, happy/unhappy, and a growing awareness of rules and behaviors in a normative sense.

An examination of children's talk and interaction between the ages of two and seven reveals the primary cognitive-affective strand of egocentricity. Conversation among peers tends to have the form of a monologue rather than of a dialogue or of discussion. A kind of mutual excitement may be generated from time to time, but there will be very little genuine exchange of ideas. In a similar way, children involved in games tend to play for themselves with disregard for the rules of others. 33 A good deal of practical intelligence is exhibited between the ages of two and seven, especially in relation to such matters as the principle of equivalence among objects or persons, but in no sense is such knowledge formalized. The principle of reversibility, which when applied to the social world has significant consequences such as generating considerations of mutuality and reciprocity, does not appear to be a part of the child's comprehension during this stage of development. However, certain cognitive acts of anticipation and reconstitution are paving the way for such understanding. 34

At the age of seven, generally speaking, there occurs a cognitive leap in development. The leap has profound implications for all levels and modes of behavior. The leap is illustrated by the sudden appearance of the principle of conservation in a child's comprehension. Prior to this stage, if a child were presented with a glass of water and a quantity of sugar, and the sugar were poured into the water where it dissolved, the child would conclude that the sugar had disappeared. Similarly, if the child were shown six strips of clay, three of which were then rolled up into balls, the child would perceive the volume of clay to have diminished as the balls were formed. In this stage the child exhibits no understanding of the principle of the conservation of matter. But at about age seven, comprehension suddenly changes. The child now understands that the sugar is still present in the glass though in a transformed state, and that the volume of clay in the balls has not changed though it has assumed a new shape. The principle of conservation can now be applied by the child to surfaces, discontinuous wholes, lengths, and so on. 35

Concurrently, a number of cognitive operations emerge full-blown. They encourage development of both logical and social structures of behavior. What happens is that during middle childhood a kind of cognitive reorganization occurs such that the child now understands relationships of objects, actions, and persons in terms of the laws of groups. For instance, numbers are no longer understood independently of each other; they are comprehended as units within the relationship of an ordered series. A particular familial relationship is comprehended as occurring within the total setting of family relations. Furthermore, the groupings are understood to be both composable and reversible. That is to say, the child now knows that several actions of the same kind can produce a third similar action, and that the total combination can be negated through disassociation. In addition to the laws of composition and reversibility, the child understands that the combining of an operation with its inverse leads to null results, and that operations can be combined in a variety of ways. With comprehension of these laws of groups, new levels of cognitive equilibrium become possible, including the structuring of mathematical and logical systems of thought.

There is a simultaneous change with regard to comprehension of social relationships as well. Flavell refers to it as the emergence of a kind of quantitative attitude, characterized by the child's belief that punishment and reward ought to be levied in proportion to what is deserved. This constitutes a distinct change from the earlier attitude which favored administering exactly the same measure of reward or punishment with no regard for such factors as intention or fairness. 36

These new characteristics are reflected in altered perceptions of mutual respect and a more mature ability to de-center or further reduce a purely egocentric perspective. Observers of children at play will discover the new attitudes at work in common understandings of rules that have been structured through interaction and so apply to all who participate. The rules may be modified for younger children who play, so that some kind of parity of opportunity is achieved. One of the most significant aspects of atti-

112

tude now to be observed is the growing willingness to hold one's own impulses and desires in abeyance in order that the objectives of a group may be achieved. We shall take a closer look at the constituents of play and the process of developing self-distance shortly, for it has much to tell us about the nature of symbolic inducement.

Before doing so, however, let us draw together what we have gleaned so far from our sojourn in the world of symbolic inducement and social interaction. Our approach has been initiated from the perspective of cognitive-symbolic principles for two simple but profound reasons. First, since all meaning and experiencing is structured in accord with the principles of cognitive activity, all meanings and experiences in the world of social behavior will, of necessity, conform to those principles. Second, the research of cognitively oriented scholars and observers has better accounted for behavior than the research of social-learning theorists. 37

Our guiding question is, how, if at all, does socialization depend on inducement by means of symbolic processes? We saw that socialization in infancy is built upon innately perceived affective states which are differentiated through various bordering behaviors such as pausing, repeating, and emphasizing. Bordering activity in this early stage of socializing indicates the innate striving for the perception of meaningful patterns which guides all behavior at any stage of sophistication. In auditory perception as well as in visual perception, the detection of pattern is essential. We saw how important rhythm was as an aid to acoustic comprehension and as a symbolic invitation to identify with and join in social interaction. The activity of both visual and acoustic systems underline the importance of the cognitive principle of perceiving and structuring boundaries. We saw that the contrast between the self and the external environment is one of the most significant boundaries to establish. The auditory system facilitates subtle and sophisticated discriminating and patterning of phenomena beyond self, thus encouraging the processes of decentering and displacement that are essential to full social development. We noted that boundaries in any form present contrast, hence choice, and so act to induce choice-making behaviors which are grounded in intent. We observed that as cognitive awareness of the autonomy of objects and others was induced symbolically, new attitudes of social awareness developed in which the individual came to identify certain of his or her interests with the interests of others, and so developed the possibilities for forming groups. All of these symbolic processes have the potential to interact with each other and to induce further symbolic behavior. Through all of this activity we saw constantly at work those principles of experiential stabilization that offer multiple or alternative meanings and experience. The import of a perceived structure

113

of meaning gets its significance from the full context of alternative possibilities. The very nature of symbolic activity, with its possibilities for denial, illusion, and fantasy, assures the fecundity of context. The world of symbolic behavior, to reiterate the words of Kenneth Burke, offers the characteristic invitation to rhetorical interaction.

THE CONSTITUENTS OF PLAY

We can see repeated and further ways in which symbolic inducement governs life if we will look at ways in which humans create and engage in deliberately constructed patterns of social interaction that they call "play." All age groups engage in "play." "Play" is social interaction under *consciously* created constraints. If we look at how people "play," we shall see a "laboratory case" of human social interaction—a case that better reflects cognitive principles and their consequences than everyday social interactions coruscated by virtue of historic and cultural influences we cannot probe. Play is created, out-of-the-ordinary behavior, the principles of which display with special clarity the characteristics of human sociality just because patterns of play are consciously created rather than simply inherited without having been examined or even, perhaps, being understood at all. Moreover, since play is *created* by those who engage in it, it is social activity in which as many human inclinations as the creators choose to include can be displayed and expressed.

Play begins in infancy with the self as the locus of all reality, and while there is a concentric enlargement of perception which induces de-centering, we never transcend ourselves completely. As Erickson points out, to follow play throughout life, one begins with the sensory systems of the body which provide the initial stimulation for pleasure, excitement, and interaction; then one moves on to the world of toys where children begin to structure knowledge regarding basic materials and arrangements of things, to the social world of playmates where personal imagination and procedure become distanced through mutual interaction to the more advanced stages of play where sides are chosen, team effort becomes important, and quasi-political dimensions of power and control become structured. 38 Through all of these stages the conception of self remains a constant principle in cognitive activity, though it undergoes transformations, because of the human need "to be central in his sphere of living rather than peripheral and ignored; active and effective rather than inactivated and helpless; selectively aware rather than overwhelmed by or deprived of sensations; and, above all, chosen and confirmed rather than bypassed and abandoned." 39

114

For those who study play, the activity very quickly loses its innocence and dimension of just sheer fun; it becomes freighted with profound meaning. From our adult perspective, we tend to regard play as an escape from the responsibilities of everyday living and as an opportunity to get recharged for the tasks that lie ahead. What we forget is that the symbolic principles involved in play are also involved in all other areas of living. They do not disappear when we move outside of the established arenas of play. As Huizinga has shown in his superb study of the human as player, elements of play can be found in such diverse activities as art and myth, philosophy and poetry, law and war, and indeed in knowing itself. What we refer to as culture can be seen to originate in play: "It does not come *from* play like a babe detaching itself from the womb: it arises *in* and *as* play, and never leaves it."40

Order and stability are significant qualities achieved by the child at play. Huizinga underscores the importance of the boundaries that demarcate play activity, boundaries of time and of space, marked off ahead of time literally or ideally, or developed as a matter of course during the activity itself.41 These boundaries function symbolically to encourage the stabilizing of certain experiences through the repetitions of behavior.

To begin with, there is the further activation of the principle of establishing boundaries within the environmental borders of play. To be alive means to move in and on the environment, to be aggressive. Erickson refers to this fundamental law of life as "aggredere," which means to "go at things."42 All of us must have enough freedom to "go at things" or we shall not reach our potential. But the going cannot occur in an unlimited fashion; physically and psychologically we must learn to live within limits, some of which are imposed upon us and some of which we must learn to impose upon ourselves. For the child, the play environment is significant in the way it encourages cognitive recognition of the function of reciprocity and the pleasures of mutuality. There comes a time when the child recognizes that in order to play together, there must be some mutual agreements reached regarding behaviors, procedures, and rules. Thus play activity invites and stabilizes commitments to convention, which result in the further ordering of experience. Willingness to commit to convention leads to an environment in which mutual expression can be sustained and mutual display can occur, both activities fostering mutual identification. The sharing of these common pleasures encourages children to experience the feelings and meanings of playmates so that a mutual appreciation for the autonomous nature of others is gained.

The commitment to conventions brings gains beyond the mutual sharing of pleasure. Through such action, behaviors are subsumed within the

115

bounds of established procedures and rules in a way that distances a child from his or her own private realm of reality. When absorbed with the procedures of play, children's thought and talk become more abstract as their personal concerns are depersonalized within the play context. Immediate rewards are delayed in deference to continuing the procedures. Anxieties and frustrations occur, but are better handled because they, too, are subsumed within the bounds of play. In all of this, in return for the exercise and development of self-discipline, the child is able to exercise some control over the situation he or she is involved in.

In play activity the structuring of boundaries occurs in three different dimensions which constitute a microcosm of the larger society. The mutual establishment of boundaries that set the relationships of the players is the core condition for interpersonal play. But it is made possible through the structuring of what Erickson calls an "inner borderline," the inner voice which urges self-constraint.[43] With the constituting of the play group, there is also established a boundary between the group and other possible groups so that in-group feelings are encouraged. Huizinga refers to this in-group atmosphere as a "feeling of being 'apart together,'" and points out that in play environments such feelings are enhanced by airs of secrecy and mystery, by disguises and other devices that set the procedures of play apart from the activities of others.[44] The very definition of group is aided by the presence, real or imagined, of alternate or opposing others. Here, in play, we see the development of attitudes and behaviors that will be utilized in the social and political structures of life.

One other feature of play must be included in our perspective. Play, says Erickson, provides the environment for "the human propensity to create model situations in which aspects of the past are re-lived, the present re-presented and renewed, and the future anticipated."[45] References to modeling lead beyond imitation, to matters of imagination and fantasy. In other words, it is not only the external world of objects and others that receives treatment in play, but the internal world of emotional states, of tension, fears, uncertainties, of ambivalent feelings, of love and hate, of destructive tendencies. There is good reason to believe that various forms of fantasy are essential to humans for the handling of psychological processes that occur beneath awareness in the tacit dimensions of experience.[46] Fantasy and imagination provide cognitive devices not only for the assimilation or purging of troublesome or ambiguous affective states, but for symbolic mechanisms to defend the ego and thwart uncomfortable experiences. Humans may use imagination and fantasy to extend and enhance experience, to transform it, and to deny it. We do not understand these cognitive maneuverings very well, but the practices of scapegoating,

the rituals of purgation, and the prevalence of myth in adult social and political life attest to the continuing presence of the symbolic functions of
fancy and fantasy, denial and defense.

Play activity, then, induces an expansion of one's concept of selfhood
through establishing and stabilizing the behaviors of relationship with
others. Play encourages one to focus on "in groups" in ways that establish
them apart from, or border them off from, other groups. And play invites
one to identify one's own interests with the interests of others in common
purpose.

SOCIAL PLAY, SOCIAL RITUAL

The play environment is obviously one that induces the stabilization of
meaning and experiencing in particular ways. The essence of play activity,
the interpersonal structuring of experience through shared conventions, is
the paradigm of social interaction; in fact, we may say it is the paradigm
of social ritual. I do not mean ritual in the ceremonial or sacred sense, although sacred ritual shares all of the same characteristics. Rather I mean
the formalizing or fixing of patterns of behavior and relationship which
serve to organize the interpersonal activities of daily living. 47 Of these
processes play is an especially clear instance. What we are interested in is
how such ritualizing activities function as modes of symbolic inducement,
and what the goals of such inducement are. In other words, through looking at play we can perhaps learn how ritualizing structures social experience rhetorically and otherwise and why it does so.

Generally speaking, of course, rules of play and ritual overcome ambiguity by structuring interaction and giving it meaning. But the purposes of
social ritual and other social play go beyond the need to organize experience, and beyond just the need to establish patterns that insure relationships with fellow beings. Play and social ritual are heavily laden with
ethical and normative commands; they stabilize behavior and meanings
with do's and don't's generated in environments that transcend individual
choice. Games and other rituals of socializing induce certain conformities
of attitude by sanctioning some modes of thought and behavior and de-
claring other modes out of bounds, unacceptable, dangerous. They function exhortatively. The exhortation does not always take explicit form; in
fact much directiveness remains implicit and out of awareness. And it is
just because of their implicit nature that the normative dimensions of
games and social rituals are so symbolically powerful.

The social world intends, as far as possible, to be taken for granted.
Socialization achieves success to the degree that this taken-for-granted

117

quality is internalized. It is not enough that the individual looks upon the key meanings of the social order as useful, desirable, or right. It is much better (better that is, in terms of social stability) if he looks upon them as inevitable, as part and parcel of the universal "nature of things."48

The symbolic nature of social ritualizing, then, is suasory in intent and rhetorical by nature. It consists partly of agreements explicitly formulated, but to a large extent it is characterized by various implicit conventions that have emerged through specific histories of human interaction. The same can be said of much other social interaction, though the details of their operations are not equally discernible.

Erickson outlines the general goals achieved through the functioning of social ritual, and what he says applies to play and to much of mundane social interaction.

1. It translates personal and individual needs and intentions into the meaning patterns appropriate to a larger group or community. It makes a virtue out of the sublimation of individuality, though, of course, it doesn't extinguish the possibilities of individuality. It identifies personal ego with the group's or community's perception of its central place in the spiritual or natural or social universe;

2. It encourages the sanctioned way of doing the simple things that comprise daily life;

3. It imposes a moral order by prescribing behavior that is acceptable and discriminating it from what is prohibited and in so doing it will encourage those cognitive habits that will continue to discriminate in the accepted pattern;

4. It places developing cognitive abilities at the service of the ideological vision shared by the group or community;

5. It provides the symbolic environment which encourges the deflection of feelings of personal unworthiness and the projection of them onto outsiders who do not conform to the sanctioned mores. In other words it encourages symbolic devices which help maintain equilibrium;

6. At each successive stage of ritualization, it encourages inducement in terms of its own symbolic form and function, thus enhancing the suasory powers of ritualistic inducement at later stages. 49

Dimensions of the rhetorical nature of ritual are identified throughout the works of Kenneth Burke, and the list of symbolic functions that can be compiled from his writings correspond with those of Erickson:

1. Ritual is a means of symbolic fixing which places idea, events, and behaviors in structures of symbolic importance;

2. Ritualistic procedures operate as means of social control by reflecting, thus perpetuating, the existing order;

3. In a similar fashion ritual enhances the persuasiveness of authority by relating those individuals who perform important roles with the functions and accomplishments of the sanctioned order;

4. Ritual can cancel certain offenses against the existing order by providing ways to scapegoat and achieve purification;

5. Ritualistic procedures can act as devices of transcendence by structuring changes in identity to accomplish a "rebirth." Erickson, too, refers to the kinds of conventions that stabilize personal identities in new ways during adolescence; 50

6. Ritual promotes mutual consubstantiality for those who participate in it. 51

The kinds of ritualistic procedures Erickson and Burke are interested in provide the subject matter of study for numerous anthropologists and sociologists. The particular forms and manifestations ritualistic procedures assume are endless and need not be catalogued here. They are illustrative of the functioning of social conventions that occur virtually at all cultural levels, in subcultures, various kinds of groups, families, at the level of interpersonal relationships of couples, and in organized play.

The fact that ritualizing procedures and social conventions take so many different forms but serve similar functions and accomplish similar objectives leads us once again to observe the extent of human diversity. We do not have a universal language system among humans; we have a multitude of differing language systems. We do not have one preferred social order or one set of conventions for inducing order. We have many different kinds of order and many different procedures for maintaining it under a multiplicity of distinguishable circumstances. Anthropologists refer to the fact of diversity within the human species as pseudo-speciation. What they mean is that humans seem to have an in-born tendency to structure experiences so that groups of individuals appear to be separate species, though in fact they are not. We identify with certain others of "our kind" so that we establish what we take to be distinct differences from "other kinds" of persons. Yet the thesis of this book, and of many other studies, is that though diverse in manners we are one in principle.

From what we have seen of the nature of cognitive activity, pseudo-speciation should not be a surprising feature of behavior. The meanings and experiences structured by mind-brain are always patterns which present the conditions of alternity. That fact, coupled with principled needs to create order and specific personal identity, leads to pseudo-speciation as a universal dimension of human existence. Erickson sums the matter up this way:

> It is only a seeming paradox that newly born Man, who could, in principle and probably within some genetic limits, fit into any number of pseudo-species and their habitats, must for that very reason be coaxed and induced to become "speciated" during a prolonged childhood by some form of family: he must be *familiarized by ritualization* with a particular version of human existence. He thus develops a distinct sense of corporate identity, later fortified against the encroachment of other pseudo-species by prejudices which can make very small differences in ritualization extraspecific and, in fact, inimical to the only "genuine" human identity. 52

Edward Wilson, too, notes the universal human tendency to divide and categorize others into kin and non-kin, members and non-members, friend and foe. We tend to fear the actions of those who are not like us, and to respond in unreasoning ways to external threats. We elevate ourselves and those like us to positions of superiority, and reduce those unlike us to an inferior status. 53 And we tend to place ourselves in the center of action and experience.

The rituals of socialization, then, induce ethical attitudes and function normatively to constrain attitudes and behaviors. They operate conservatively to encourage the maintenance of "acceptable" behaviors. In the variety of their manifestations they undergird and further encourage the natural human tendency to pseudo-speciate.

The tendency to pseudo-speciation is encouraged in the play environment and by ritual where dimensions of distancing and bordering are induced. Distancing begins with the individual who subordinates self to the conventions of a group and thus becomes identified with the group. Both personal constraint and freedom are experienced by anyone who makes immediate selfish gratification secondary to the goals and activities of the group on the one hand and makes gaining a sense of enhancement through group participation primary. The player, ritualist, or other proceduralist escapes alienation, and through abiding by the conventions of a group is freed of disorder and ambiguity and is able to share in the control of group activity. Throughout all of social life, individuals are similarly involved in maintaining this dual relationship between personal ego and identification within various structures of group activity. The consequences depend on how social experience is symbolized and what behaviors the symbolization induces. As Mary Douglas indicates, excessive distancing from self, through subordination to a group, can lead an individual to place excessive stock in the boundaries of the group and to guard group boundaries emphatically against external threat. And the opposite can happen.

Should personal ego so predominate that an individual feels uncommitted to and unbound by group identification, there will be excessive, perhaps punishing, concern for internal feeling states.[54] A healthy relationship is achieved through maintaining an equilibrium between self and group whether the field of action be play, ritual, or mundane social engagements.

SOCIAL INDUCEMENT AND SOCIETY

A second dimension of social bordering occurs in the structuring of a group's identity over and against those who are non-members or by contrast with other groups. Now can arise the larger societal structures in which groups function cooperatively or competitively. Thus we come to the kinds of identifications and divisions that characterize cultural and intercultural structures. At this high level of social interaction the principle of contrast and alternity that governs the sensory systems of the body produces its analogue in societal pseudo-speciation. This is the level of experience Kenneth Burke treats extensively as a fundamental source of rhetorical behavior. It is a perceptual world in which affirmations of identifications and inducements to identifications are important just because of the constant possibilities of division: "Identification is affirmed with earnestness precisely because there is division. If men were not apart from one another, there would be no need for the rhetorician to proclaim their unity."[55]

Burke argues that the possibilities and focuses of division induce possibilities and hopes for identification. But we can make equal sense by reversing the equation. Identification can only be meaningful amidst diversity; alternity and opposition are essential for the experiencing of meaning, beginning with the basic cognitive activity of structuring as it is conducted by the sensory systems and continuing through all aspects of meaning constructed within organized symbol systems, ending in the forms of pseudo-speciation necessary for establishing a sense of social being and belonging. What we need to notice is that perceptions of ambiguity, instability, and disorder invariably exist alongside urgencies for security, predictability, and coherence. The former are not always insidious. A shake-up of an existing social order can lead to transformations and new syntheses that are creative and productive both personally and socially. The same can be true within intimate personal relationships. But, of course, the opposite is always possible, and states of excessive disequilibrium can culminate in what Burke refers to as the ultimate "disease" of cooperation: war at the broadest social level[55] and insanity at the personal, private level.

121

The symbolic ability to gain distance from self, to de-center and displace, enables humans to join together in common causes and to submit to the ordering principles of social groups, but the same ability also enables us to disassociate from groups and to disobey the conventions of order. Fear of disorder and a pervasive need to avoid chaos lead to the structuring of institutions and conventions and to constant production of symbolic inducements for their maintenance. It is for this reason that Geertz suggests that we shall not understand culture clearly if we perceive it as complexes of behavior patterns such as traditions, customs and usages; we need to see culture as "a set of control mechanisms—plans, recipes, rules, instructions—for the governing of behavior." 57

The specific manifestations of these universal organizing principles vary, of course, in response to such factors as geography, cultural heritage, and concrete cultural preference. But, in relation to social interaction and order, two principles are continually stabilized and encouraged: submission of individual will and gratification to the larger communal welfare, and the security and maintenance of boundaries against the unwarranted incursions and alien "natures" of alternative groupings and cultures. Activity in accord with these principles thoroughly imbues social structures with inducements of and toward moral certitude and piety. As Havelock observed, "the profound feeling that violation has been imposed upon a normative order and that this is unseemly and unfitting and untraditional, and that the cure lies in a return of propriety, responds to the deepest instinct of preliterate man." 58 His statement applies equally to literate societies, for the feeling he identifies is rooted in the principled ways mind-body does and must structure experience symbolically.

Burke, too, describes social ordering in a way that illustrates transformation of personal perceptions of self as the center of experience and reality to the socio-cultural level. As Burke outlines the process, humans develop forms of governance and structures of social status just as they construct the boundaries, categories, and hierarchies that constitute their formulations of "nature." In consequence qualities of moral grandeur can be projected upon their social constructions for "nature is man's servant, and man is nature's sovereign." On the same principle social designs can become mythically sanctified if and when constructions of "nature" presuppose a supernatural order that decrees social order according to supernatural principles. Presupposition of a supernatural order is ideationally, hence symbolically and hierarchically, prior to construction of the social order "to the extent that it [the supernatural order] sums up all the *principles* felt to have been guiding the socio-political order." 59 Burke is saying that symbolically constructed supernatural orders derive from symbolically constructed "lesser" orderings, but that, being summative and having superiority projected upon them, the now sanctified designs acquire directive force relative to mundane socio-political ordering.

Burke's description leads to consideration of the kinds of symbolic ordering referred to as "myth" or "ideology" or "social vision." No matter what label is used, this ultimate form of rhetorical ordering follows the principles of mind-brain activity and fulfills significant social functions. It sanctions particular principles of order by placing them under the aegis of a piously charged design. It encompasses inconsistencies and contradictions of motive through obscurantism and mystification. It sanctions purgative symbolic strategies of projection, transformation, and reduction. It impregnates social convention with normative and moral imperatives. It offers multiple possibilities for personal identification through presenting meaning structures flexible enough to encourage reinterpretation in response to viscissitudes of time and fortune. Above all, it provides an ultimate synthesis of experience, an all-encompassing boundary for the structuring of vagrant meaning. It prescribes the border that separates those who are centrally engaged in the "right way" of existence from those who are not.

Though they promise fulfillment for idealistic compulsions in pursuit of completion and perfection, ideological and mythic visions are, of course, but partial views. They present only single ways, among alternatives, of "knowing" the universe of experience. Because they are partial, they are partisan; each can offer but one mode of specifying the neurophysiological tendencies inherent in humans. Each must, therefore, feature symbolic inducements of cognitive defense that are the certain marks of individuality and pseudo-speciation.

If we turn from such all-encompassing ways of structuring social experience, as ideology represents, to less encompassing evidences of bordering-fixing principles of symbolic processing, we can find manifestations of the pervasive human urge for pseudo-speciation. For instance, language functions to encourage exclusivity and divisiveness. By use of grammatical structure, word choice, inflection, and accompanying gesture, intimate compatriots, secret societies, recreational and professional groups, and social and ethnic classes affirm their identities and posture against alternative life styles. Following the principle of bordering, the richest uses of language are more private and concealing than open and disclosive, more personal than public. Steiner reflects on this matter:

> We speak first to ourselves, then to those nearest us in kinship and locale.
> We turn only gradually to the outsider, and we do so with safeguard of
> obliqueness, of reservation, of conventional flatness or outright misgui-

> dance. At its intimate center, in the zone of familial or totemic immediacy, our language is most economic of explanation, most dense with intentionality and compacted implication. Streaming outward it thins, loosing energy and pressure as it reaches an alien speaker. 60

In-group language and behavior help structure and maintain the identifications of "we-ness" and "group-ness." These individuated "accents," says Steiner, are worn like coats of arms, operating like instruments of inclusion and exclusion. They are at once constitutive and divisive. 61 In-group language functions such as these reinforce a point made earlier in the book: we shall be mistaken if we take linguistic behavior to be exclusively or even fundamentally communicative. It is constitutive as well as reflective òf fundamental bordering-fixing brain processes.

Steiner concludes that the agonistic functions of speech are extremely important, serving to structure social boundaries and thereby preserve social life. They are, he says, "defensive adaptations, body painting, the capacity of the leaf-moth to take on the coloration of its background." 62

> At every level, from brute camouflage to poetic vision, the linguistic capacity to conceal, misinform, leave ambiguous, hypothesize, invent, is indispensable to the equilibrium of human consciousness and to the development of man in society. Only a small portion of human discourse is markedly veracious or informative in any monovalent, unqualified sense. The scheme of unambiguous propositions, of utterances as direct pointers of homologous responders to a preceding utterance, which is set out in formal grammars and in the extension of information theory to language study, is an abstraction. It has only the most occasional, specialized counterpart in natural language. In actual speech all but a small class of definitional or "unreflective-response" sentences are surrounded, mutely ramified, blurred by an immeasurably dense, individualized field of intention and withholding. Scarcely anything in human speech is what it sounds. Thus is it inaccurate and theoretically spurious to schematize language as "information" or to identify language, be it unspoken or vocalized, with "communication." The latter term will serve only if it includes, if it places emphasis on, what is *not* said in the saying, what is said only partially, allusively or with intent to screen. Human speech conceals far more than it confides; it blurs much more than it defines; it distances more than it connects. The terrain between speaker and hearer—even when the current of discourse is internalized, when "I" speak to "myself," this duality being itself a fiction of "alternity"—is unstable, full of mirage and pitfalls. 63

The bordering-fixing principles that generate ideology and its accompanying language with special focus on groupness and divisiveness not only allow, but in linguistic action encourage and fix socially counterfactual behavior perhaps even more than the principles encourage and fix factuality. Thus we see the social significance of the counterfactual tendencies of language discussed in Chapter 3, and we can appreciate their role in the realm of symbolic inducement.

Contrasting and bordering are essential to the healthy working of mind-brain. The autistic patient is unable to recognize or formulate the boundary between himself and the other constituents of his environment. The schizophrenic cannot maintain adequate boundaries either, and thus is unable to focus on relevant experiences in order to initiate coherent behavior. [64] Perception of contrast and structuring of borders lead to creation of meaningful patterns of experience; they are key factors, though not the only ones, in the maintenance of cognitive equilibrium. They are the shapers of cogency, coherence, and comprehension. Contrasting and bordering also create the possibilities of relationship and the corresponding principles of conservation, reversibility, equality, autonomy, proportion, and mutuality that make social existence and action possible. These principles, when operative in the malleable stability of social convention, give coherence and efficiency to social interaction. They generate and help maintain social equilibrium, which is not synonymous with social equality. These cognitive social principles and the overt behaviors they induce shape what we refer to as partnership, opposition, and diversity.

In social shaping there is inevitably systematic distortion of whatever we may suppose "objective" reality to be. Humans are not equipped to resonate to all possibilities in the environment. And, as I have shown above, the human need for self-protection leads us to mask, transform, or deny possibilities we might resonate with. The limits and principles of human symbolic processing make it difficult to say what social "distortion" is and is not.

The manifestations of convention and control that we impose and submit to in our social environment are multitudinous and subject to endless variation. They are the external manifestations of the processes of self-control that we employ to segregate and subdue or conserve our personal and private natures. We must therefore include within our purview the inducements imposed upon us not only by others, but by ourselves, "in varying degrees of deliberateness and unawareness, through motives indeterminately self-protective and/or suicidal." [65]

It can be argued that symbolic social shaping is what induces most people to continue to live. The most portentous of our masquerades is our ignoring of, and therefore denial of, our own mortality. We go on living and planning as though by some genetic loophole we might escape our own inevitable demise. As Karl Scheibe says,

> Our own death is, after all, not empirically certain, for it has never been observed to happen. It is merely a deduction from the collocation of ma-

jor and minor premises, and either premise might be challenged by our stock of inner sophistries. At a certain level, however, the knowledge is there without benefit of syllogism or demonstration. By not allowing that knowledge to speak, by forcing it into muteness, we succeed in holding secrets from ourselves. 66

George Steiner surmises that without capacities for symbolic counterfactuality and alternity, the human species would not have evolved to its present status; it would have self-destructed along the way. "It is in this respect that human tongues, with their conspicuous consumption of subjunctive, future, and optative forms, are a decisive evolutionary advantage." 67 Steiner is wise enough to see the contribution of such terms as more constructive than merely deceiving. Through our habits of thought, through the principles on which we structure the world, we are able to proceed in the "substantive illusion of freedom." To this I would add a modified reprise of a comment made in the earlier discussion of mindbrain: We "know" our reality as we are equipped, and as we wish, to know it. Midgley caps the reprise:

. . . an individual depends for this satisfaction on the repertory of tastes native to his species; he cannot jump off his feet. What is special about people is their power of understanding what is going on, and using that understanding to regulate it. Imagination and conceptual thought intensify all the conflicts by multiplying the options, by letting us form all manner of incompatible schemes and allowing us to know what we are missing, and also by greatly increasing our powers of self-deception. 68

What we have glimpsed in this chapter are ways in which cognitive principles become operationalized in socialization. Just as the principles of cognition function actively to structure our experiencing in order that we can understand and cope with our environment, so we move to structure and comprehend our interpersonal interactions and social relations with others. We undertake behaviors that have social consequences. Our behaviors are inevitably guided by purposes and choices, though we are not always fully conscious of them. We identify with other like-minded fellows and against those we perceive to be dissimilar fellows and thus build the structures of society, which in turn operate to further constrain us in reflexive ways.

William Burch asserts that "Unlike nature, the web of human society is woven of myth and rhetoric, of faith and persuasion, which filter and sort the meanings of man and nature." 69 It is natural that most of us are responsive to others of our kind, bcause of our similar symbolizing natures. Our symbolizing invites other symbolizing in answer. We are born, with abilities and capacities to symbolize already in place, into an environment that is already heavily structured symbolically. These symbolic structures are not fashioned willy-nilly, nor out of whole cloth. They are a natural reflection of the symbolic nature of humans. We are, thereby, socially induced to develop our own capacities fully in individuated ways. In other words, we enter and mature in a world that is rich with symbolic invitations to action. We make choices following the constraints of our cognitive principles. We are induced to seek and impose order on our interactions with others. We build patterns of social association. We stabilize and repeat patterns of behavior that prove efficacious. In identifying ourselves with the interests and efforts of some, we inevitably divide ourselves from others. We commit to those interests and are in turn further induced and constrained by them. We symbolize in ways that we hope will affect and effect the symbolizing of others. They, in turn, so symbolize to us. Symbolizing has the capacity to sustain, modify, or alter further symbolizing and thus, the structures of human relationship. We are simultaneously symbolic and social beings.

NOTES

1. Midgley, 96.
2. Edward O. Wilson, *On Human Nature* (Cambridge: Harvard University Press, 1978), 18.
3. Geertz, 44. See especially 44–51 for Geertz' complete statement.
4. Eric H. Lenneberg, *Biological Foundations of Language* (New York: John Wiley and Sons, 1967), 473–74.
5. Raymond Wilson, *The Long Revolution* (London: Cox and Wyman, Ltd., Pelican Books, 1965), 117.
6. Daniel Stern, *The First Relationship* (Cambridge: Harvard University Press, 1977), 81. See also Lee C. Lee, *Personality Development in Childhood* (Monterey, California: Brooks/Cole Publishing Co., 1976), 58. Experimental work which confirms the conclusion can be found in R. Fantz, "Visual Perception for Birth as Shown by Pattern Selectivity," *Annals of the New York Academy of Science*, 118 (1965), 793–815, and J. Kagan, B. A. Henker, J. Levine, and M. Lewis, "Infants' Differential Reactions to Familiar and Distorted Faces," *Child Development*, 37 (1966), 519–32.
7. In the discussion of caregiver/infant interaction that follows I have drawn heavily upon Stern. See especially pp. 13–107.
8. Ibid., 103.
9. Frank E. X. Dance. "The Acoustic Trigger to Conceptualization: An Hypothesis Concerning the Role of the Spoken Word in the Development of Higher Mental Processes," paper presented at the Annual Meeting of the American Association for the Advancement of Science in Washington, D.C., February 16, 1978, 1–16. The discussion here relies heavily upon Dance's descriptive account.

10. For corroborating evidence, see P. H. Wolff, "Observations on Newborn Infants," *Psychosomatic Medicine*, 21 (1959), 110–18; P. D. Eimas, E. R. Sequeland, P. Jusczyk, and J. Vigorito, "Speech Perception in Infants," *Science*, 171 (Jan. 22, 1971), 303–06; P. E. Eimas and J. D. Corbit, "Selective Adaptation of Linguistic Feature Detectors," *Cognitive Psychology*, 4 (1973), 99–109; D. L. Molfese, "Cerebral Asymmetry in Infants, Children and Adults: Auditory Evoked Responses to Speech and Noise Stimuli," unpublished doctoral dissertation (The Pennsylvania State University, 1972); P. A. Morse, "Infant Speech Perception: A Preliminary Model and Review of the Literature" in R. L. Schiefelbusch and L. L. Lloyd, eds., *Language Perspectives—Acquisition, Retardation and Intervention* (Baltimore: University Park Press, 1974), 19–53.

11. P. D. Eimas, "Speech Perception in Early Infancy," in L. B. Cohen and P. Salapatek, eds., *Infant Perception: From Sensation to Cognition* (New York: Academic Press, 1975).

12. Dance, 4–5.

13. Ibid., 6.

14. Ibid., 7.

15. Kenneth Burke, *A Rhetoric of Motives* (New York: World Publishing Company, Meridian Books, 1962), 548.

16. Stern, 90.

17. Lenneberg, 117. Parentheses are Lenneberg's. For his full discussion see pp. 107–20.

18. Ibid., 119.

19. M. F. Berry, *Language Disorders of Children* (New York: Appleton-Century-Crofts, 1969), 38–39.

20. Condon.

21. A. R. Luria, *Higher Cortical Functions in Man* (New York: Basic Books, 1966), 102.

22. M. T. Turvey, "Preliminaries to a Theory of Action with Reference to Vision," In Shaw and Bransford, eds., *Perceiving, Acting, Knowing*, 258–59.

23. T. Halwes and B. Wire, "A Possible Solution to the Pattern Recognition Problem in the Speech Modality," In W. B. Weimer and D. S. Palermo, eds., *Cognition and the Symbolic Processes*, 387–88.

24. A. M. Liberman, F. S. Cooper, D. P. Shankweiler, and M. Studdert Kennedy, "Perception of the Speech Code," *Psychological Review*, 74, No. 6 (November 1967), 453.

25. J. S. Bruner, "Origins of Mind in Infancy," paper presented at meeting of the American Psychological Association, September 1967, 7–8.

26. Lenneberg, 279–81.

27. Ibid., 387.

28. Roger Brown, *A First Language* (Cambridge: Harvard University Press, 1973), 167–68, 410.

29. My guide for the discussion of cognitive development in the child is a concise presentation of Piaget's views, "The Mental Development of the Child," which appears in *Six Psychological Studies*, 3–73. Readers who want a more fully elaborated discussion of Piaget's perspective should see his *The Origins of Intelligence in Children*, referred to earlier, *Play, Dreams and Imitation in Childhood* (New York: Norton, 1951), and *The Construction of Reality in the Child* (New

York: Basic Books, 1954). While there has been some quibbling with the age ranges Piaget attributes to certain stages of development, his general outlines of the stages are accepted by most.

30. *Six Psychological Studies*, 15.

31. John H. Flavell, *Cognitive Development* (Englewood Cliffs, N.J.: Prentice-Hall, 1977), 122–23.

32. For a more comprehensive discussion of the stages of moral development that I follow in this discussion, see L. Kohlberg, "Stage and Sequence: The Cognitive-Developmental Approach to Socialization" in D. A. Goslin, ed., *Handbook of Socialization Theory and Research* (New York: Rand McNally, 1969). While paralleling Piaget's stages, Kohlberg's have not yet received enough sustained research attention to establish them in relation to Piaget's.

33. Piaget, 20–21.

34. Ibid., 33.

35. Ibid., 46.

36. Flavell, 123.

37. Lee, 148.

38. Erik H. Erickson, *Toys and Reason* (New York: W. W. Norton, 1977), 68–69.

39. Ibid., 49.

40. Johan Huizinga, *Homo Ludens* (Boston: Beacon Press, 1960, 2nd ed.), 173. Emphasis in original.

41. Ibid., 9–10.

42. Erickson, 56.

43. Ibid., 59.

44. Huizinga, 12.

45. Erickson, 44.

46. See Bruno Bettelheim, *The Uses of Enchantment* (New York: Random House, 1975).

47. Huizinga draws the direct parallel between play and ceremonial ritual; 18–19. Erickson discusses ritualizing activity in its daily context, and I am following the general lines of his treatment.

48. Peter Berger, "Religion and World Construction," in Dennis Brisset and Charles Edgley, eds., *Life as Theatre* (Chicago: Aldine Publishing Company, 1975), 239. Parentheses and quotation marks are Berger's.

49. Erickson, 82–83. I have paraphrased and modified Erickson's list but have remained consistent with his discussion.

50. Ibid., 106–10.

51. For a more thorough examination of Burke's views on the rhetoric of ritual, see Cynthia M. Danel, "The Relationship of Rhetoric and Ritual as Discussed in the Major Works of Kenneth Burke," unpublished Master's thesis, (Pennsylvania State University, 1976).

52. Erickson, 79–80. The italics are Erickson's.

53. Wilson, 70.

54. Mary Douglas, *Natural Symbols* (New York: Pantheon Books, 1970).

55. Burke, 546.

56. Ibid., 546.

57. Geertz, 44.

58. Havelock, *The Greek Concept of Justice*, 35.

59. Burke, *The Rhetoric of Religion* (Boston: Beacon Press, 1961), 240–41. Italics are Burke's.

60. Steiner, 231.

61. Ibid., 32.

62. Ibid., 226.

63. Ibid., 229. The quotation marks and italics are Steiner's.

64. See *Language and Thought in Schizophrenia*, J. S. Kasamin, ed., (New York: W. W. Norton, 1964), and Brendan A. Maher, "Shattered Language of Schizophrenia," *Psychology Today*, Vol. 2, No. 6 (November 1968), 33.

65. Burke, *A Rhetoric of Motives*, 559.

66. Karl E. Scheibe, *Mirrors, Masks, Lies and Secrets* (New York: Praeger Publishers, 1979), 98.

67. Steiner, 227.

68. Midgley, 282–83.

69. William Burch, *Daydreams and Nightmares* (New York: Harper and Row, 1971), 9.

5

RHETORIC AS
SYMBOLIC INDUCEMENT

We come to the end of our search for the principles of symbolic induce-ment. Now, the tasks are to synthesize the major ideas and concepts dis-cussed in earlier chapters, to explain the nature of the phenomena called rhetoric, and to consider the implications of what has been said for those who wish to understand human rhetorical activity. No new theory of rhe-toric emerges from the data that have been reviewed, but I hope to show that what has been said renders rhetoric more intelligible as an aspect of symbolic behavior. By argument and example I shall undertake to show that to study human activity as *rhetorical* activity is to inquire into the ac-tual and potential functions of principled symbolic *inducement*. I shall ar-gue that exploration of *rhetoric* comes about when one asks a certain kind of question about ubiquitous symbolic activity. We must begin by review-ing the nature of symbolic behavior in humans.

SYMBOLIC BEHAVIOR

The most fundamental conceptualization that underlies study of rhe-torical behavior is that humans are, as Kenneth Burke has said, symbol-using, symbol-making, symbol-misusing beings.1 From what has been said to this point we can appreciate what this means. All that we experi-ence, all that we "know," all of the meaning we create and respond to is made possible by our innate capacity to symbolize. It is *all* symbolic be-havior. Our neurophysiological processing is always and inevitably geared to structure our experiencing symbolically, and basic but complex principles of mind-brain activity guide and shape all of the symbolizing we engage in.

At the most basic level, all neuronal firing is in response to motor cen-ters in the brain and is patterned firing. Single cells never fire alone, but al-ways in conjunction with other cells. The firing action is both positive and negative; that is, when certain combinations of cells fire they simulta-neously suppress the possible firing of other patterns. When a pattern fires, it lowers its own firing threshold so that, on the next similar stimulus occasion, it is likely to fire again. Further, the basic or primary pattern of firing will, in turn, trigger secondary or following patterns of firing, all levels of firing being ordered by the motor centers of the brain. The com-plexity of this basic activity becomes apparent when we realize that the same pattern of neuronal firing can be a primary pattern at one time and a part of secondary or following patterns at another. And neuronal cells can

131

function as motor centers at one time but as parts of a pattern responding to motor-center commands at another time.

This basic process was detailed earlier. I recall it here because the process functions according to principles that have direct analogues in what is called cognitive processing. Whether cognitive processing occurs at the level of consciousness or outside of our awareness, it consists of actions that structure or pattern our experiencing. Structuring occurs through the mind-brain's resonating with structures in the external environment and/or within the mind-brain itself. Cognitive structures are holistic, and they gain richness of meaning within the larger context of other structures that associate with them. Thus, all normal experiencing is systematized or ordered in some fashion. Put in different terms, principles of mind-brain activity stabilize stimuli-in-flux by producing certain kinds of choices, providing boundaries that create unities of experience, inducing the association of other unities of experience, and systematizing unities on the principle of hierarchic order. As we have seen throughout our exploration, the processing and structuring activity described here is rhythmic activity.

Two other principles must be added to structuring activity. Structuring activity always operates on the principle of abstraction. All experiencing, all perceiving, all knowing is selective. Not only is it the case that we face our own neurophysiological limits so that we cannot perceive all there is to be perceived, but we choose not to perceive all that we can. Characteristically, symbolic fixing is deflective as well as directive; one of the important functions of cognitive processing is the activity of cutting away or shutting out certain stimuli so that the mind can operate efficiently and with greater emotional balance and comfort. Symbolic structuring then, is always an abstractive process, involving selection, choice, and purpose. We choose from among those stimuli available to us, thus structuring our "realities from among alternatives." Our most basic patterns of neural firing are abstractions as are our most sophisticated systems of mathematics, and all of our experiencing in between.

Closely allied with the principle of abstraction is that of classification. Classification is the act of searching for and detecting similarities and differences and deciding what shall be grouped with what. We saw earlier that mind-brain imposes categories on perceived phenomena, and that it engages in multiple classifications simultaneously. The classifications become more and more abstract with each phase of processing. Once again, selection, choice, and purpose are involved.

Here we have fundamental principles of cognitive processing that underlie all symbolic experiencing and production: bordering or the structuring of boundaries, rhythm, association, abstraction, categorization, and hierarchy. I do not claim that this list is exhaustive. I do not know; nor does anyone. Investigators are just beginning to learn about several unfamiliar aspects of brain function. And, as Hayek pointed out, we shall never know all there is to know because we have no more powerful instrument by which to understand the brain than the brain itself. I do claim, however, that the neurophysiological-cognitive principles I have identified are agreed upon as fundamental and universal by those who are most expert in such matters.

In explaining fundamental processes of cognition, I have used the terms "choice," "intention," and "induce." Each term implies that decisions about alternatives occur. The question logically arises, then, whether principles of cognition are principles of inducement toward one decision or another. If that were the case, could the concept of rhetoric, as "symbolic inducement," be distinguished from such concepts as psychology or neurophysiology? My answer is that the question of whether principles of cognition are principles of inducement is wrongly posed. We must remember that principles of cognition function in more ways than one. *One* of those functions is inducement, the function appropriately associated with rhetorical experience. I shall discuss this matter in more detail shortly.

My immediate point is that from the initial act of perceiving and structuring "data" to any subsequent, overt, physical action taken in light of perceptions, all human experiencing is symbolic. "Reality" is symbolic reality. That is all we have. Our comprehension of how the world works and how we should function in relation to it is dependent on how our brains are organized to process the contents of our experiencing. For reasons already given, to state the matter in this way is not to be reductive in any simple sense. Our brain is a sophisticated, flexible, highly resourceful instrument.

We cannot be sure that we know all of the functions of cognition, but we are aware of some of them, and we know enough about them to be able to discuss them:

1. All cognitive activity functions as an act or as action. The brain is not passive, but moves upon the environment in accord with its own principles.
2. Cognitive activity functions to manifest purpose. At all stages of cognition, from the tacit or out-of-awareness stage to the conscious and most explicit stage, intention and purposing are involved in a central way.

3. Closely related is the function of manifesting choice. All cognitive activity is involved with making determinations from among alternative symbolic realities.

4. Cognitive activity functions to stabilize symbolic realities through structuring and relating. All normal human experiencing is bounded and shaped so that meanings can be stabilized.

5. Cognition functions to achieve self-awareness and self-identification. The achievements of this function develop over time in the maturing child and are realized in greater or lesser degree.

6. Cognition functions to maintain equilibrium. Thus, a large share of cognitive activity may be involved with "symbolic compensation" in one form or another.

7. Cognitive action functions to induce symbolically. It is this dimension of cognitive action that yields experience we may properly call rhetorical experience.

All of these principles of cognition must be understood to operate in the manner of closed-feedback-loop action. This is to say that all of the principles of cognition are interactive, mutually influencing and mutually supporting one another in greater or lesser degree. Thus, the "tenor" of the total interaction is continuously subject to modification, depending on which principle or principles are most salient. These cognitive principles function conjointly to achieve comprehension, which includes states of feeling and emotion, in order that we may act within our environments.

THE NATURE OF SYMBOLIC INDUCEMENT

Throughout our exploration of symbolic behavior we have been uncovering and examining various manifestations of symbolic activity that induces. Symbolic activity that induces is activity that invites, lures, or guides us on to action within and in response to the environment. At the end of Chapter 2, I identified six principles that give rise to inducement: "edging" or bounding, rhythm, association, classification, abstraction, and hierarchic ordering. It is now possible to say, in general terms, how these principles work within the various specific contexts in which they operate.

1. Symbolic activity induces by imposing order. We strive to avoid ambiguity and the unknown; we seek to comprehend holistically. Symbolic processing is directed toward achievement of closure and completion along whatever symbolic pathway we follow. This

means that at the most fundamental levels of symbolic processing our perceptions will be continuous even though the phenomena being perceived are intermittent. It means that at more sophisticated levels of processing we will construct ideologies—holistic and encompassing systems of explanation of how the "world" works or how it ought to work. Either kind of activity and all comparable activity invites, lures, or guides toward action.

2. Symbolic activity is guided by associational patterns of symbolizing, patterning that occurs in response to initial acts of structuring. An important part of the meaning of any symbolic structure or pattern derives from the larger context in which the structure is perceived and understood. At fundamental levels of symbolic processing "following patterns" of neuronal firings always accompany initial patterns of firing. At more sophisticated levels of processing perceptual "models" are constantly being compared with relevant portions of our larger cognitive "maps" of "reality." At ideological levels of processing, explanations of phenomena that posit chance or accident or idiosyncratic features will not seem efficacious.

3. Symbolic actions induce their own likely recurrence when similar conditions arise. Symbolic structures, once formed, are not necessarily and rigidly parts of ongoing brain processing, but such structures create tendencies toward their reuse. And the more a given structure is relied on, the more permanent that structure is likely to become. At fundamental levels of brain activity we have seen that the firing of a neuronal pattern lowers its firing threshold so that under similar circumstances that pattern is encouraged again. At more sophisticated levels of processing, cognitive maps of "reality" become relatively stable and slow to change. At ideological levels of processing we will be much more likely to try to fit new stimuli into already constructed systems of explanation than to be changed by the stimuli. Even distortion of stimuli may occur in order to create a "fit."

4. Symbolic actions guide perceptions and thus behaviors. Intention, purpose, and choice making are involved at all stages of symbolic processing. We not only perceive *this* phenomenon rather than *that* phenomenon, but we choose to see the phenomenon in *this* particular way rather than in *that* particular way. Symbolic processing always induces partisanship in perception. For example, visual perception rests on the principle of contrast rather than other conceivable principles. At sophisticated levels of processing we always identify ourselves with sets of interests, goals, and explanations,

135

eschewing alternatives. And we will behave according to the partiality of our perceptions.

5.   Human symbolic behavior tends to attract and induce response from other similarly behaving beings. We are all invited to achieve satisfaction through symbolic processing because it is our nature to process symbolically. *My* symbolic processing, with its partisan symbolic content, invites *you* to achieve satisfaction by processing "data" similarly in order to attain holistic grasp of self and environment. Thus, shared constructions of "reality" are created, monitored, and "verified."

These aspects of symbolic inducement operate in the manner of a closed feedback loop. They operate together in mutually interactive, influential, and supportive ways, the tenor of the interaction being always subject to change with changes in the saliency of what is being experienced.

RHETORIC AS SYMBOLIC INDUCEMENT

Having seen some of the ways in which inducement occurs as a consequence of symbolic processing in mind-brain, we can now ask what *rhetoric* is, according to the analyses developed in this book. I presuppose that the term *rhetoric* cannot be usefully defined as coextensive with the phrase *human behavior*. If that is accepted, then what aspect or aspects of behavior fall within the purview of what we may choose to call rhetoric? Early in this book I accepted a definition of rhetoric asserting that rhetoric is the study of human symbolic inducement. With analyses of mind-brain, of symbolic processing, and of inducement before us, we can perhaps see what it is to study human symbolic inducement and how such study can be carried out.

If the study of rhetoric is concerned with analysis and understanding of symbolic inducement, rhetoric is obviously not to be identified with any particular kind of messages or meanings. We have seen that symbolic inducement is always involved in all human symbolic behavior; therefore, the inducement that rhetoric is concerned with is present in all messages and in all meaning. Given this, the question of rhetoric's relationship to knowing becomes a specious question, for the rhetorical function of inducing is a part of all knowing.

I pointed out in Chapter 1 that context determines what we are willing to accept as knowledge. What stands as "knowledge" in the sciences, and the criteria for determining such knowledge, differ from content and criteria of that which stands as "knowledge in ethics or aesthetics. However, the human symbolic processes that underlie all "knowing" are the same, and all areas of knowledge and all criteria for determining "knowledge" are symbolic constructs. Since the principles of symbolic inducement operate in all symbolic processes of knowing, rhetoric is not to be associated only with some areas of knowledge. If rhetoric is the study of symbolic inducement, that which rhetoric studies is present in every kind of knowledge. Neither can rhetoric, as study of symbolic inducement, be identified with any set of procedures, or rules, or methods. Insofar as procedures, rules, and methods have meaning, the rhetorical function of symbolic inducement will inhere in all of them.

The goal of such scholarship is presumably to comprehend rhetorical behaviors more fully. To explore how rhetoric, as symbolic inducement, works and with what consequences is a task to which almost every so-called "discipline" can contribute. In exploration of this sort it will not do to conceive of discrete areas or domains of study, as we might legitimately do when thinking about the study of geography or plant science. A student of rhetoric is not identified by the artifacts studied nor by the methods used to conduct the study. A student of rhetoric is identified by the question he or she raises about symbolic behavior. That question is: What are the actual or potential functions of symbolic inducement and what are the actual or potential consequences of those functions? This point informed a statement made more than a decade ago concerning the nature of rhetorical criticism: "Rhetorical criticism may be applied to any human act, process, product or artifact which, in the critic's view, may formulate, sustain, or modify attention, perceptions, attitudes, or behavior."[2]

To define study of rhetoric as study of symbolic inducement with a view to understanding its actual and potential nature and consequences may seem unduly inclusive, but the focus of a student of rhetoric is in fact specific. That this is true can be shown by examining some examples of how expert students of rhetoric have looked or could look at symbolic phenomena. To illustrate how the *way of looking* defines rhetorical study, I shall include among my examples objects for study that may not, at first, seem likely candidates for rhetorical analysis. Few would question the claim that all oral and written statements are open to study as symbolic inducements. Clearly, such statements have potential for rhetorical impact. Neither would there be much dispute about exploring televised and filmic presentations for their rhetorical qualities. Gestures and other nonverbal behaviors are similarly candidates for rhetorical study. It is not equally obvious that music or other fine arts invite rhetorical exploration, but all have rhetorical potential. Some music, of course, is clearly ideological or propagandistic, but insofar as any music, through rhythmic or tonal qual-

137

ity, can induce certain moods or attitudes in a listener, it is rhetorical. Likewise, insofar as a painting invites us to see its subject in a particular way, or the techniques of an artist can lead our eyes to a particular location on a canvas, the principles of symbolic inducement are at work. I shall not draw my examples from any of these instances of human creativity and communication. To emphasize the pervasiveness of symbolically inducing rhetorical phenomena, I shall initially illustrate what rhetorical study is by considering the study of mathematics, the art of interior design, and the sport of football.

Let us begin with mathematics. Here is a very precise science. Its problems and procedures, its formulae and equations and sets, deal with certainties and precisely calculated probabilities. To be sure, those certainties and probabilities are internal ones; that is, they are confined within the systems that produce them. But they are certainties and calculated probabilities nonetheless. How then can there be inducement, involving choice, in a symbol system that does not seem to allow choice? The answer is the system itself; the inevitability and elegance of both system and its results can be the inducement. It is the beauty of mathematics that can be the lure.

It is interesting to read in a biography of newspaper correspondent and political analyst Walter Lippmann that there might have been another career he would have enjoyed:

> Years later, when asked if he had even been tempted to choose a different profession, he said that he might have enjoyed being a mathematician— if he had had the talent. "I would have liked that kind of life. the precision—the elegance—there's something about it that attracts me aesthetically." 3

Lippmann revealed clearly what is symbolically inducing about mathematics for many who study it.

Lord Bertrand Russell, who was among other things a philosopher and social critic, was also a mathematician. His *Principia Mathematica* is one of the classics in the history of mathematical study. As Russell himself declares, his interest in mathematics went beyond what math, itself, can do:

> Mathematics rightly viewed, possesses not only truth, but supreme beauty—a beauty cold and austere, like that of sculpture, without appeal to any part of our weaker nature, without the gorgeous trappings of painting or music, yet sublimely pure and capable of stern perfection such as only the greatest art can show. The true spirit of delight, the exaltation, the sense of being more than man, which is the touchstone of highest excellence, is to be found in mathematics as surely as in poetry. 4

One can be interested in the study of mathematics for a variety of reasons. One might be concerned with the development of theoretical mathematical systems, with the practical applications of theoretical concepts, with the advantages of one system of geometry over another, or with the modes of thought required by mathematical systems. Interests such as these do not necessarily beckon the rhetorical focus. But when terms like "aesthetic," "beauty," "appeal," and "sublimely pure" turn up in discussions about mathematics, they invite the practiced eye of a student of rhetoric, for they reveal the manifestations of the principles of symbolic inducement.

While we are on the subject of mathematics, consider geometry. Our visual perceptions of the external environment undergo a stage of neural activity in which they are processed in terms of straight parallel lines because of the way input channels from the primary light-receptors of the retina hook up to the brain. Consequently, a geometry based on straight parallel lines and plane surfaces is the most compatible with the principles of the mind. Says Stent:

> Thus neurology has shown why it is human—all too human—to hold Euclidean geometry and its nonintersecting coplaner parallel lines to be a self-evident truth. Non-Euclidean geometries of convex or concave surfaces, although our brain is evidently capable of perceiving them, are more alien to our built-in-spatial-perception processes. Apparently a beginning has now been made in providing, in terms of cellular communication, an explanation for one of the deepest of all philosophical problems; the relation between reality and the mind. 5

What I conclude from these remarks is that we are induced to be more accepting of and comfortable with Euclidean geometry by very fundamental principles of cognitive activity. I also conclude that "induced" is exactly the right term to use, because Stent himself poses the possibilities of alternity that can exist among geometric systems.

Let us next turn to interior design and decoration. When one is considering how to outfit and order a room, there are a number of concerns that may arise. Given the function of the room, what will be necessary to furnish it? Given those items, what will be the most efficient arrangement? Are there little extra touches that might add "class"? What color combinations will be most pleasing? These last two concerns are becoming more rhetorical, whereas the first two do not necessarily include rhetorical concerns. But the last two have to do with the meanings that can be conveyed by the way a room is furnished and the way items in the room relate together. We know, if we but stop and think about it, that thought is often given to what a doctor's office or a psychiatrist's office should look like, to look official, to convey a sense of credibility and trustworthiness, and so on. These are rhetorical concerns having to do with the possibilities of symbolic inducement.

One of the leading law firms in the country is Covington and Burling. Joseph Goulden provides a description of the firm's Washington, D.C., office. The description is riddled with the rhetorical overtones of the place and the people who work in it:

> To reach the inner sanctum of Covington and Burling, Washington's premier law firm, one rides the elevator to the seventh floor of the eighty-story office building at 888 16th Street Northwest, across Lafayette Park from the White House, and steps into the subdued ambience of old and dignified money. The living room is that of a very, very tasteful home, its furnishing so congruous with the light-hued wood paneling that, think as you may the next day, not a single individual piece comes to memory. A constant—and most silent—flow of lawyers (all wearing coats and ties and *white* shirts) and secretaries over the carpeted floor, figures whose silence detaches them one from the other, heads bobbing politely in the general direction of the receptionist, lips rippling into what *could* be a smile. Dignity. Covington and Burling people, be they lawyer or functionary, do not banter. They hold their file folders snugly under their arms, and they do not swing their briefcases as they walk to the elevator and (Blackstone forbid!) the secretaries do not chew gum or carry lighted cigarettes or come to work bra-less. Not a glance at The Visitor, for when someone enters Covington and Burling, regardless of his business, he is entitled to privacy, and thus one must ignore even the existential fact that The Visitor is sitting in open view on the sofa. Walk on, silently and briskly, and close the door behind you. 6

"Ambience," "Dignity." These are terms that refer to rhetorical impact, to the kinds of attitudes and behaviors that can be elicited by the furnishings and settings in a room. There are principles of symbolic inducement working in an environment like this, just as surely as in a campaign speech or a televised advertisement, and a student of rhetoric may search them out and examine them.

It is obvious from Theodore White's description of the oval office during John F. Kennedy's presidency, that principles of inducement function in the White House:

> The tones of the room are as perfect as its proportions. The gray-green expanse of carpeting, into which is woven the Great Seal of the United States, is keyed to the same pastel tonality as the cream-beige walls and the beige draperies. The room changes somewhat from President to President, as it has changed from Eisenhower to Kennedy. Where in Eisenhower's time the room possessed an uncluttered, almost overpower-

ing openness as one approached the seven foot, four inch dark walnut desk at which Eisenhower . . . sat, it has been softened now with two new curving cream-white sofas before the fireplace that invite the visitor to a respectful closeness with the President. 7

The word, "invite" is White's term, of course, and it indicates the way he felt when he visited the oval office; it refers to a part of the meaning the setting and decor evoked in him. But that is precisely where such symbolic invitations are experienced, in the perceptions and meanings people hold in their heads. At minimum, we have to say the Oval Office functioned rhetorically, among other ways, on Theodore White.

Finally, consider football. More specifically, let us concentrate our focus on the defensive alignment of a football eleven. As football fans know, the defensive formations of a team are based on the positions of linemen, linebackers, and defensive halfbacks and safeties. By the end of a season, a fan can talk knowledgeably about whether a team has a good pass rush, is capable of stopping wide running plays, gets tough in its goal line stands, has the speed to stop an opponent's long passing game, and other similar matters. Football coaches develop more specialized interests in what a defense can do. For instance, if a defensive end splits out a foot and a half wider from the tackle than he usually does, is he in a better position to stop a roll-out quarterback? If the linemen hit the gaps in the opposing line rather than taking on their opponents head-on, do they have a better chance to sack the quarterback? What defensive formations are best against the power runner, against the short pass, against a long crossing pass pattern, and so on? There are a host of such concerns that come with growing sophistication of the game.

But there are also principles of symbolic inducement at work in a defensive formation, and they are of interest. If a linebacker is positioned close to the line at the outset of a play so that the opposing quarterback perceives what appears to be an open zone for passing behind the linebacker, and if at the start of a play the linebacker fakes forward, but rushes backward to fill the once unoccupied zone, and intercepts the pass, the symbolic inducement of the defensive alignment has done its job. If a defensive team runs a series of formations that utilize man-to-man pass coverage, then suddenly slips into a formation that looks the same at the outset of a play but turns into a zone pass defense as the play develops, then the principles of symbolic inducement are alive and operating on the football field. When coaches put together game plans that they hope will fool the opposition, or will induce the opposition to try certain kinds of plays, or will "hide" a weak aspect of the defensive team, the coaches' considerations are rhetorical in a straightforward way. I do not know of a rhetorical critique of a football game, but if a critic knew what to look for, a rhetorical critique could be produced.

A student of rhetoric is identified by and limited by the focus that guides his or her investigation. The questions asked and the answers obtained are specific to the study of rhetoric. They arise from the assumptions and concepts of symbolic activity that have emerged in the course of this investigation. The root assumption is that one of the dimensions of human symbolic activity is inducement—of self and others. As long as anyone focuses on this feature of symbolization, that person functions as a rhetorical analyst, regardless of the phenomena studied.

The gains of a rhetorical focus on phenomena are enriched and strengthened by thorough understanding of human symbolic behavior. To know the principles of such behavior and how they function is to know what to look for and how to interpret what one uncovers, because all behavior is grounded in and constrained by those principles. Such knowledge can enable an analyst to look below the surface of an event to discover the subtle, inner workings of inducement that are present. The kinds of knowledge such inquiries can produce are illustrated in the work of a number of rhetorical scholars. A few instances of such work will clarify the point I am now making.

As an extended illustration of what rhetorical inquiry yields as knowledge, I cite Hermann Stelzner's analysis of Franklin Roosevelt's "War Message," delivered to the Congress the day after Pearl Harbor was attacked. Stelzner undertakes close textual analysis, an approach he terms "topographical."

> The speech is the "particular place" and, to assess the configuration of its language, its "road," "rivers," "cities," "lakes," and "relief" are examined. To shift the figure, fragments of language are not selected from the speech and regarded as dominant lights, independent and autonomous. The concern is with the constellation, not the major stars alone. Interest centers on the order, movement, meanings, and interrelations of the language; the object is to discover not only what goes on, but how it goes on. The aim is full disclosure. 8

Stelzner does look thoroughly at all of the language in the speech and at the interrelationships of the language. But as we shall see, he goes beyond the language to examine the rhetorical manifestations of some of the symbolic processes we discussed earlier.

At one point in his essay Stelzner focuses on the following lines in Roosevelt's speech:

> Yesterday the Japanese Government also launched an attack against Malaya. Last night Japanese forces attacked Hong Kong. Last night Japa-

142

nese forces attacked Guam. Last night Japanese forces attacked the Philippine Islands. Last night Japanese forces attacked Wake Island. And this morning the Japanese attacked Midway Island.

Stelzner's exegesis of these lines takes note of the way several linguistic and presentational features share a structural correspondence with the events Roosevelt describes:

> . . . the verb "launched" more than attacked; it launched a series of sentences which structurally (i.e., in form) harmonize with the acts imbedded in them. The actions (i.e., their substance) and the manner of describing them (form) are one. 9

The "last night" series is briefly discussed in relation to the semantic context preceding it. Then the critic says:

> Finally, the stress which the language contributes, sustains, and intensifies the general emphasis of the "last night" passage. "Yesterday" has three syllables, the first being accented. The phrase "last night" has two accented syllables, relatively equal in stress. Each "last night" is encircled by "attack" or "attacked." The stress pattern of the language is a bombardment. The final line begins with a conjunction which readies the listener for the final "to top it all off." This "and," too, is a term of some stress and strength. "And this morning," a phrase of four syllables, the first three accented, concludes the bombardment. 10

Stelzner then goes on to show that alternative descriptions would have resulted in a less satisfactory pattern of meaning.

Let us be precise about what the critic is focusing on when he describes the way Roosevelt's sentences correspond structurally with the actions they describe. The key lies in our understanding of the critical emphasis on "pace" and "stress." These are terms that refer to certain tonal qualities of the message, to oral, aural features of the message. Through the employment of pacing and stress, a speaker orally produces a rhythmic pattern; in this case the rhythmic pattern structures the aural image of bombardment. If one listens to a tape recording of Roosevelt delivering the speech to Congress and the nation, one can readily affirm Stelzner's astute insight into the inducing qualities of rhythm in this portion of the message. He has correctly captured the aural comprehension of Japanese military action that one experiences by listening to the rhythmic patterning of Roosevelt's delivery.

Stelzner's insightful commentary emphasizes the fact that our criticism of oral symbolization may be impoverished to an extent by the neglect of such phenomena of oral presentation as rhythm. Earlier, we examined evidence showing how fundamental rhythm is to brain activity and language development. We saw Havelock's discussion of the significant role rhythm played in the memory and presentation of the bard in oral culture. Rosenberg discovered that there are occasions when rhythm plays a vital role for both speaker and listener in our culture; in addition to aiding recall it invites participation and emotional involvement, helping to establish an environment in which the audience can respond. 11 Rhythm, then, becomes rhetorically significant in its own right.

Burke has one of the most direct discussions of the rhetoric of rhythmic form:

> . . . we know that many purely formal patterns can readily awaken an attitude of collaborative expectancy in us. For instance, imagine a passage built about a set of oppositions (*we* do *this,* but *they* on the other hand do *that; we* stay *here* but *they* go *there; we* look *up,* but *they* look *down,* etc.). Once you grasp the trend of the form, it invites participation regardless of the subject matter. Formally, you will find yourself swinging along with the succession of antithesis, even though you may not agree with the proposition that is being presented in this form. 12

It is not difficult while reading this statement to recall the effectiveness of antithetical forms in Kennedy's inaugural address, a speech memorable enough to have a place already in our country's anthology of patriotic literature. Rhythm is what Burke is referring to in a way that emphasizes its potential to function as symbolic inducement. More directly related to our interests here, Stelzner implicitly raises the relationship of rhythm to perspective and comprehension, explicitly he answers the question.

In further discussion of Roosevelt's terminology, Stelzner emphasizes the subtleties of symbolic forming. He explicates a line Roosevelt delivers immediately following the announcement of the Japanese attack on Pearl Harbor. The line is: "In addition, American ships have been reported torpedoed on the high seas between San Francisco and Honolulu." Stelzner points out that the "news" of the sentence is alarming, but that Roosevelt has muted the alarm by the placement of his phrasing.

> The language moves danger "away from" the shores of the United States. The proper nouns, San Francisco and Honolulu, are necessary to the overall effect. Let the speaker say: *In addition, American ships have been reported torpedoed on the high seas.* Responses become: Where? Everywhere? Close to the United States? How close? Distant? How distant? The proper nouns meet some of the questions. Where? On a direct path between San Francisco and Honolulu. One can almost see it on the wall map of the mind—the narrow, well-defined shipping route. Close? How close? Ambiguously the image suggests movement *away* from. One may speculate on the range of possible responses had the speaker said, *on the high seas between Honolulu and San Francisco,* or merely, *on the high seas.* 13

Stelzner's analysis is alive to the possibilities of ambiguity in an ambiguous situation, as well as to the hopes and fears of the American audience. And while he fully respects the "fixing" potential of the words Roosevelt chose, he also demonstrates that the meaning of the sentence clearly moves beyond the literal wording. The words make no explicit mention of the direct and restricted shipping lane between San Francisco and Honolulu, but Stelzner shows how such imagery might be evoked in one's mind. Nor is there any logic of grammar or meaning that I know of, that would lead one to the impression that the submarine attacks were distanced from America's shores. But Stelzner's discussion of that pattern of meaning refers to reasonable possibilities of symbolic inducement, given the exigencies of the moment.

In another portion of his analysis, Stelzner describes the way associated patterns of meaning are induced by words that evoke a particular kind of imagery. He refers to Roosevelt's identification of the enemy forces as "Japanese air squadrons":

> "Japanese air squadrons" were the instruments of attack. The phrase might have been rendered: *after the Japanese air force or after Japanese air forces.* These alternatives parallel better the first reference to the Japanese military; but therein lies a weakness. The modified repetition provides some variety. More important is the matter of image. *Air force* and *air forces* denote and connote mass, a large quantity which blankets a sky. Such a mass moves, but in droning and lumbering fashion. "Air squadrons" is a sharper definable form of the force, as an image in the mind's eye. The image is of small groups, of well-defined patterns in the total mass, of tightly knit units sweeping in and out over the target.
>
> "Air squadrons" is quantitative, definitive, and repetitive. To the extent that squadrons are patterns, the image presents formal patterns inflicting damage. 14

Here Stelzner shows not only that a particular pattern of meaning has the potential to evoke additional related patterns, but that such patterns will always invite experiencing in a particular way. Earlier, we saw that in brain activity the firing of any neuronal pattern will induce the firing of related neuronal patterns. And we saw that experiences are always induced in selective and partisan ways; we experience in *these* kinds of ways rather than in *those* kinds of ways.

There is more we could say about Stelzner's critical analysis, including some things we might add based on what we know about symbolic behavior. For instance, we might notice the power Roosevelt gains from concrete imagery that, as Stelzner remarks, easily induces "pictures" in the mind, remembering as we do so the special force such imagery enjoyed in oral cultures. While the invention of writing surely provides a significant

145

technological overlay that induces certain nuances of meaning, it is likely that vivid, concrete imagery can impress us just as it did our preliterate ancestors. We might also wonder if Roosevelt gains by using terms that refer to visual perception, as he does when he says, "There is no blinking at the fact that our people, our territory and our interests are in grave danger," recalling that our visual sensory system has been crucial for our survival as a species. But we have done enough with Stelzner's critique to appreciate how the nature of human symbolic behavior, as described in this book, allows Stelzner to draw the analytical conclusions he does.

For a brief example of the critical uncovering of symbolic inducement we turn to Thomas Benson's close textual analysis of Frederick Wiseman's documentary film *High School*. Benson points out that through the use of his filmic medium Wiseman is inviting his audience to experience a certain complex of meanings concerning institutional power in a high school. *High School* is in the tradition of cinema verité, and its scenes of classrooms, halls, gymnasium, students, teachers, and administrators capture some of the events of high school that viewers can closely identify with. But Wiseman does not intend a neutral presentation. Benson's critical thesis is that *High School* invites viewers to experience the structural relations of the themes of power and sexuality and the subordinate manifestations of these themes that appear in distorted interpersonal communication, twisted languages, confused identities, militarism, and boredom.[15] He conducts a close, frame-by-frame analysis of the film, scrutinizing shot composition, juxtaposition of imagery, portrayal of character, interplay of dialogue, and so on. He uncovers the vehicle of inducement that Wiseman uses throughout the film:

> . . . the repetition of sexual elements, and the way they are placed in context, is likely to predispose the viewer to decode them in something like the way I am describing. But I must strain the reader's credulity further by arguing that the sexual material works on the viewer of the film much as it works on the student in the school: for the student, it exists as part of the double-bind that reinforces the school's power while remaining just at the edge of consciousness. And for the film viewer the sexual material is also usually just out of conscious awareness, inviting us to feel angry about the power of the school without quite realizing why we are so angry.[16]

To arrive at his critical conclusions, Benson draws upon his knowledge of the medium of film, his expertise at delineating and explaining rhetorical inducement, and his understanding of human perception; combining these resources, he describes Wiseman's argumentative perspective on the uses of social convention and relationship to mold attitude and behavior.

146

In that portion of his analysis referred to just above, when Benson talks of matters of inducement that are just "out of conscious awareness," he is operating on the principle that tacit dimensions of experiencing can be as potent with regard to constraining our perception as the experiencing we are keenly aware of. Earlier, we saw tacit dimensions operating in visual perception, in language acquisition, in the understanding of the rules of set theory, and in the interpersonal relationships of play, to mention a few areas of interest.

In an essay by Campbell and Jamieson concerning the factors which can coalesce to give rise to generic rhetoric, the authors discuss such matters as the influence of conventions, universal and cultural stereotypes, previous rhetorical acts, and others. Their essay is one of the most sensible and useful written on rhetorical genre, for they clearly indicate what kinds of insights into human behavior may be gained through generic criticism. They suggest that the theory "underlying the concept of genre is critical theory, theory about the enterprise of criticism." Of course, this is correct as far as it goes, but one can go further to describe it also as a theory about a fundamental aspect of human nature and symbolic inducement. In fact, Campbell and Jamieson say as much:

> . . . it [generic criticism] seeks to recreate the symbolic context in which the act emerged so that criticism can teach us about the nature of human communicative response and about the ways in which rhetoric is shaped by prior rhetoric, by verbal conventions in a culture, and by past formulation of ideas and issues. 17

Both of these scholars have presented us with criticism that illustrates the point. Let me take just one example. Following the American Revolution President Washington faced uncertainties growing out of the fact that despite twelve years of life under the Articles of Confederation, the most familiar governmental forms derived from monarchy. Among existing uncertainties was what relationship should obtain between President and Congress under the new constitution. Earlier debate about the presidency had shown a strong majority opinion against any trappings of monarchy. Yet one of the first interactions between President Washington and the Congress consisted of Washington's presenting a speech that closely resembled the "King's Speech," traditionally delivered by the monarch to the Parliament. The congressional response was similar to the traditional "echoing speech" that constituted Parliament's customary reply to the King. As Jamieson points out, despite the intense desire to avoid mimicking the English crown, reversion to form on this occasion is readily understandable. There was no native American tradition to provide ritualized forms of executive-legislative relationship, and in such moments of uncer-

147

tainty and ambiguity it is typical for humans to turn to past, familiar behaviors that have proved efficacious in analogous circumstances.[18]

Here we have an example in the forming of social conventions that reflects the normal proclivity of the human mind when confronting uncertainty. Those structures and patterns that have been cognitively stabilized will act as inducements to assert order and predictability in an ambiguous environment—at times even inappropriately. The general cognitive principle operating here leads to conservative behavior in times of stress. This tendency can even become exacerbated under conditions of crisis, resulting in regression to infantile behavior.[19] Jamieson has pointed to a public manifestation, mild in comparison to infantile regression, of behavior grounded in individual neuropsychology. The early American executive-legislative exchange was an example of "human communicative response" based on "fundamental human needs."

Other instances of enlightening rhetorical analysis could be cited, but those I have just reviewed show how a rhetorical focus on communicative events can bring the processes of symbolic inducement into the open even though the rhetorical interactions examined are very different. Jamieson reveals how once-established structures of symbolic forming have potential to induce subsequent behavior in keeping with their intrinsic natures. The observation identifies a practical consequence of the fact that the firing of a neuronal pattern can encourage and reinforce its repetition, if similarities of environment and internal state are perceived. Stelzner uncovers the way the rhythms of vocal presentation tap into basic rhythms of cognitive activity and, in an emotionally charged context, can evoke comprehension with moral judgment at its core. Benson shows how fundamental tendencies can become clothed in conventions of social interaction that can then be presented in a symbolic medium to prompt emotion and attitudes directively.

Students of rhetoric as symbolic inducement will never arrive at an exhaustive description of the genre of argumentation or the characteristics of performative rhetoric. Completion of such tasks is as unattainable as generating a finite model of a system of language. But insofar as they elucidate manifestations of symbolic inducement as conformances to stabilized cognitive principles, those who study rhetoric will elucidate rhetoric's function in human knowing.

Inducement is inherent in all symbolic activity, though it is not all there is to symbolic activity. In general terms, symbolic inducement operates as "lure," "goad," "enticement," "invitation," leading us to become consubstantial with particular modes of symbolizing. Symbolic inducement offers promise of satisfaction, gained from participating in symbolizing and from the outcomes of symbolizing. The principles of such inducing begin in cognitive activity that structures experiencing. Those principles operate within the systems of symbols that are constructed to create, modify, and manipulate knowledge and behavior. And the same principles function in the manifestations of social interaction that are pertinent to knowledge and behavior. The study of rhetoric is the study of symbolic inducement as it manifests itself in neurophysiological, cognitive, and social levels of human activity.

NOTES

1. Kenneth Burke, *Language as Symbolic Action* (Berkeley, University of California Press, 1966), 6.
2. "Report of the Committee on the Advancement and Refinement of Rhetorical Criticism" in Lloyd F. Bitzer and Edwin Black, eds., *The Prospect of Rhetoric* (Englewood Cliffs, N.J.: Prentice-Hall, 1971), 220.
3. Ronald Steel, *Walter Lippmann and the American Century* (New York: Random House, 1980), 496.
4. Bertrand Russell, *Mysticism and Logic* (London: George Allen and Unwin, 1917), 60.
5. Gunther S. Stent, "Cellular Communication," *Scientific American,* 227 (September, 1972), 51.
6. Joseph C. Goulden, *The Superlawyers* (New York: Dell Publishing Co., 1973), 25. Parentheses and italics are Goulden's.
7. Theodore H. White, *The Making of the President, 1960* (New York: Atheneum Publishers, 1961), 371.
8. Hermann G. Stelzner, " 'War Message,' December 8, 1941: An Approach to Language" in Robert L. Scott and Bernard L. Brock, *Methods of Rhetorical Criticism* (New York: Harper & Row, 1972), 290, 291.
9. Ibid., 302.
10. Ibid., 302, 303.
11. Bruce A. Rosenberg, *The Art of the American Folk Preacher* (New York: Oxford University Press, 1970). See especially pp. 17, 76–78, and 105.
12. Burke, *Rhetoric of Motives,* 582.
13. Stelzner, 300.
14. Ibid., 297.
15. Thomas W. Benson, "The Rhetorical Structure of Frederick Wiseman's *High School, Communication Monographs,* 47 (November 1980), 241.
16. Ibid., 241.
17. Karlyn Kohrs Campbell and Kathleen Hall Jamieson, "Form and Genre in Rhetorical Criticism: An Introduction," in Campbell and Jamieson, eds., *Form and Genre: Shaping Rhetorical Action* (Falls Church, Va.: The Speech Communication Association, n.d.), 26–27.
18. Kathleen Hall Jamieson, "Antecedent Genre as Rhetorical Constraint," *Quarterly Journal of Speech,* 61 (December 1975), 411–14.
19. Taylor, 111.

BIBLIOGRAPHY

Alexander, I. W. *Bergson: Philosopher of Reflection.* New York: Hilary House, 1957.

Arnheim, Rudolf. *Visual Thinking.* Berkeley: University of California Press, 1969.

Bartlett, F. C. *Remembering: A Study in Experimental and Social Psychology.* Cambridge: Cambridge University Press, 1932.

Benson, Thomas W. "The Rhetorical Structure of Frederick Wiseman's *High School."Communication Monographs,* 1980, 47, pp. 233–61.

Berger, Peter, "Religion and World Construction." In Dennis Brisset and Charles Edgley (eds.), *Life as Theatre.* Chicago: Aldine Publishing Company, 1975.

Berry, M. F. *Language Disorders of Children.* New York: Appleton-Century-Crofts, 1969.

Bettelheim, Bruno. *The Uses of Enchantment.* New York: Random House, 1975.

Bickerton, Derek. *Roots of Language.* Ann Arbor: Karoma Publishers, 1981.

Bitzer, Lloyd F. and Edwin Black (eds.). *The Prospect of Rhetoric.* Englewood Cliffs, N.J.: Prentice-Hall, 1971.

Blakemore, C. "Developmental Factors in the Formation of Feature Extracting Neurons." In O. Schmitt and F. G. Worden (eds.), *The Neurosciences Third Study Program.* Cambridge: MIT Press, 1974.

Bohm, David. "Science as Perception-Communication." In F. Suppe (ed.), *The Structure of Scientific Theories.* Urbana: University of Illinois Press, 1974.

Booth, Wayne C. *Modern Dogma and the Rhetoric of Assent.* Notre Dame: University of Notre Dame Press, 1974.

Bransford, J. D. and N. S. McCarrell. "A Sketch of a Cognitive Approach to Comprehension: Some Thoughts About Understanding What It Means to Comprehend." In W. B. Weimer and D. S. Palermo (eds.), *Cognition and the Symbolic Processes.* Hillsdale, N.J.: Lawrence Erlbaum Associates, 1974.

Bransford, J. D., J. R. Barclay, and J. J. Franks. "Sentence Memory: A Constructive Versus Interpretative Approach." *Cognitive Psychology,* 1972, 3, pp. 193–209.

Bransford, J. D., and Jeffery Franks. "The Abstraction of Linguistic Ideas." *Cognitive Psychology,* 1971, 2, pp. 331–50.

Brewer, W. F. "The Problem of Meaning and Higher Mental Processes." In Walter Weimer and David S. Palermo (eds.). *Cognition and the Symbolic Processes.* Hillsdale, N.J.: Lawrence Erlbaum Associates, 1974.

150

Brown, J. *Mind, Brain, Consciousness: Neurophysiology of Cognition.* New York: Academic Press, 1977.

Brown, Roger. *A First Language.* Cambridge: Harvard University Press, 1973.

Brown, Roger W. "Language and Categories." In Jerome S. Bruner, Jacqueline J. Goodnow, and George A. Austin, *A Study of Thinking.* New York: John Wiley & Sons, 1956.

Brown, R. W. and E. H. Lenneberg. "A Study in Language and Cognition." *Journal of Abnormal Social Psychology,* 1954, 59, pp. 454–62.

Brummett, Barry. "Some Implications of 'Process' or 'Intersubjectivity': Postmodern Rhetoric." *Philosophy and Rhetoric,* 1976, 9, pp. 21–49.

Bruner, J. S. "Origins of Mind in Infancy." Paper presented at American Psychological Association Convention, September, 1967.

Burch, William. *Daydreams and Nightmares.* New York: Harper & Row, 1971.

Burke, Kenneth. *A Grammar of Motives and a Rhetoric of Motives.* Cleveland: World Publishing Company, 1962.

_____. *Language as Symbolic Action.* Berkeley: University of California Press, 1968.

_____. *The Rhetoric of Religion.* Boston: Beacon Press, 1961.

_____. *A Rhetoric of Motives.* New York: World Publishing Company, Meridian Books, 1962.

Campbell, Karlyn Kohrs and Kathleen Hall Jamieson, "Form and Genre in Rhetorical Criticism: An Introduction." In Karlyn Kohrs Campbell and Kathleen Hall Jamieson (eds.), *Form and Genre: Shaping Rhetorical Action.* Falls Church, Va.: Speech Communication Association, n.d.

Carleton, Walter M. "What Is Rhetorical Knowledge: A Response to Farrell—and More." *Quarterly Journal of Speech,* 1978, 64, pp. 313–28.

Cassirer, Ernst. *The Logic of the Humanities.* Trans. by Clarence Smith Howe. New Haven: Yale University Press, 1961.

_____. *The Philosophy of Symbolic Forms. Volume One: Language.* New Haven: Yale University Press, 1975.

_____. *The Philosophy of Symbolic Forms. Volume Two: Mythical Thought.* Trans. by Ralph Manheim. New Haven: Yale University Press, 1974.

_____. "Reflections on the Concept of Group and the Theory of Perception." In Donald Phillip Verene (ed.), *Symbol, Myth and Culture: Essays and Lectures of Ernst Cassirer, 1935–1945.* New Haven: Yale University Press, 1979.

Bibliography

Cherwitz, Richard. "Rhetoric as 'A Way of Knowing': An Attenuation of the Epistemological Claims of the 'New Rhetoric'." *Central States Speech Journal,* 1977, 42, pp. 207–19.

Dance, Frank E. X. "The Acoustic Trigger to Conceptualization: An Hypothesis Concerning the Role of the Spoken Word in the Development of Higher Mental Processes." Paper presented at the Annual Meeting of the American Association for the Advancement of Science, Washington, D.C., February 16, 1978.

Danel, Cynthia M. "The Relationship of Rhetoric and Ritual as Discussed in the Major Works of Kenneth Burke." Unpublished master's thesis. Pennsylvania State University, 1976.

Dodds, E. R. *The Greeks and the Irrational.* Berkeley: University of California Press, 1951.

Douglas, Mary. *Natural Symbols.* New York: Pantheon Books, 1970.

Eccles, J. J. *The Brain and the Unity of Conscious Experience.* Cambridge: Cambridge University Press, 1965.

Eimas, P. D. and J. D. Corbit. "Selective Adaptation of Linguistic Feature Detectors." *Cognitive Psychology,* 1973, 4, pp. 99–109.

Eimas, P. D. "Speech Perception in Early Infancy." In L. B. Cohen and P. Salapatek (eds.), *Infant Perception: From Sensation to Cognition.* New York: Academic Press, 1975.

Eimas, P. D., E. R. Sigueland, P. Jusczyk, and J. Vigorito. "Speech Perception in Infants." *Science.* 1971, 171, pp. 303–6.

Erickson, Erik H. *Toys and Reason.* New York: W. W. Norton, 1977.

Fantz, R. "Visual Perception from Birth as Shown by Pattern Selectivity." *Annals of the New York Academy of Science,* 1965, 118, pp. 793–815.

Farrell, Thomas B. "Knowledge, Consensus and Rhetorical Theory." *Quarterly Journal of Speech,* 1976, 62, pp. 1–14.

_____. "Social Knowledge II." *Quarterly Journal of Speech,* 1978, 64, pp. 329–34.

Fillenbaum, S. "Memory for Gist: Some Relevant Variables." *Language and Speech,* 1966, 9, pp. 217–27.

Flavell, John H. *Cognitive Development.* Englewood Cliffs, N.J: Prentice-Hall, 1977.

Geertz, Clifford. *The Interpretation of Cultures.* New York: Basic Books, 1973.

Gibson, James J. *The Ecological Approach to Visual Perception*. Boston: Houghton Mifflin, 1979.

_____. *The Senses Considered as Perceptual Systems*. Boston: Houghton Mifflin, 1966.

_____. "What Gives Rise to the Perception of Motion?" *Psychological Review*, 1968, 75, pp. 335–46.

Giuliani, Allessandro. "Vico's Rhetorical Philosophy and the New Rhetoric." In G. Tagliacozzo and D. P. Verene (eds.), *Giambattista Vico: New Science of Humanity*. Baltimore: John Hopkins University Press, 1976.

Goody, Jack and Ian Watt. "The Consequences of Literacy." *Comparative Studies in Society and History*, 1963, 5, pp. 304–45.

Goody, Jack. *The Domestication of the Savage Mind*. Cambridge: Cambridge University Press, 1977.

Goulden, Joseph C. *The Superlawyers*. New York: Dell Publishing Company, 1973.

Grassi, Ernesto. "Can Rhetoric Provide a New Basis for Philosophizing? The Humanist Tradition." *Philosophy and Rhetoric*, 1978, II, pp. 75–97.

_____. "Rhetoric and Philosophy." *Philosophy and Rhetoric*, 1976, 9, pp. 200–16.

_____. *Rhetoric as Philosophy: The Humanist Tradition*. University Park: Pennsylvania State University Press, 1980.

Gray, H. *Anatomy*. London: Longmans, 1973.

Gregory, Richard L. *Eye and Brain*. New York: McGraw-Hill, 1978.

_____. *Mind in Science*. Cambridge: Cambridge University Press, 1981.

Gurin, Joel. "Chemical Feelings." *Science 80*, 1979, pp. 28–32.

Halwes, T. and B. Wire. "A Possible Solution to the Pattern Recognition Problem in the Speech Modality." In W. B. Weimer and D. S. Palermo (eds.), *Cognition and the Symbolic Processes*. Hillsdale, N.J.: Lawrence Erlbaum Associates, 1974.

Hamilton, Edith and Huntington Cairns (eds.). *Phaedrus*, 265 and 266. In *Plato: The Collected Works*. New York: Bollingen Foundation, 1961.

Hanson, Norwood Russell. "A Picture Theory of Theory Meaning." In Robert Colodny (ed.), *The Nature and Function of Scientific Theories*. Pittsburgh: University of Pittsburgh Press, 1970.

Bibliography

Hauser, Gerard A. and Donald P. Cushman. "McKeon's Philosophy of Communication: The Architectonic and Interdisciplinary Arts." *Philosophy and Rhetoric,* 1973, 6, pp. 211–34.

Havelock, Eric A. *Origins of Western Literacy.* Ontario: Ontario Institute for Studies in Education, 1976.

_____. *Preface to Plato.* Cambridge: Harvard University Press, 1963.

_____. *Prologue to Greek Literacy.* Cincinnati: University of Cincinnati Press, 1971.

_____. "The Alphabetization of Homer." In Eric A. Havelock and Jackson P. Hershbell (eds.), *Communication Arts in the Ancient World.* New York: Hastings House, 1978.

_____. *The Greek Concept of Justice.* Cambridge: Harvard University Press, 1978.

Hayek, Friedrich A. *The Sensory Order.* Chicago: University of Chicago Press, 1976.

Hilgard, Ernest R. "Neodissociation Theory of Multiple Cognitive Systems." In Gary E. Schwartz and David Shapire (eds.), *Consciousness and Self-Regulation.* New York: Plenum Press, 1976.

Hirsch, H. and D. N. Spinelli. "Distribution of Receptive Field Orientation: Modification Contingent on Conditions of Visual Experience." *Science,* 1970, 168, pp. 869–71.

Hubel, David H. "The Brain," *Scientific American,* 1979, 241, pp. 45–53.

Hubel, David H. and Torsten N. Wiesel. "Brain Mechanisms of Visions." *Scientific American,* 1979, 241, pp. 150–62.

Huizinga, Johan. *Homo Ludens.* Boston: Beacon Press, 1960

Hyde, T. S. and J. J. Jenkins. "Recall of Words as a Function of Semantic, Graphic, and Syntactic Ordering Tasks." *Journal of Verbal Learning and Verbal Behavior,* 1973, 12, pp. 471–89.

Itzkoff, Seymour. *Ernst Cassirer, Scientific Knowledge and the Concept of Man.* Notre Dame: University of Notre Dame Press, 1971.

Jamieson, Kathleen Hall. "Antecedent Genre as Rhetorical Constraint." *Quarterly Journal of Speech,* 1975, 61, pp. 406–15.

Jeffrey, L. H. *The Local Scripts of Archaic Greece.* Oxford: Oxford University Press, 1961.

Jerison, Harry J. "Paleoneurology and the Evolution of Mind." *Scientific American,* 1976, 234, pp. 90–101.

Johanson, Donald and Maitland Edey. *Lucy: The Beginnings of Humankind.* New York: Simon and Schuster, 1981.

Johansson, G. "Visual Perception of Biological Motion and a Model for Its Analysis." *Perception and Psychophysics,* 1973, 14, pp. 201–11.

Kagan, J., B. A. Henker, J. Levine, and M. Lewis. "Infants' Differential Reactions to Familiar and Distorted Faces." *Child Development,* 1966, 37, pp. 519–32.

Kandel, Eric R. "Small Systems of Neurons." *Scientific American,* 1979, 241, pp. 66–76.

Kasámin, J. S. (ed.), *Language and Thought in Schizophrenia.* New York: W. W. Norton, 1964.

Katz, J. J. *Semantic Theory.* New York: Harper & Row, 1972.

Katz, J. J. and J. A. Fodor. "The Structure of a Semantic Theory." *Language,* 1963, 39, pp. 170–210.

Kohlberg, L. "Stage and Sequence: The Cognitive-Developmental Approach to Socialization." In D. A. Goslin (ed.), *Handbook of Socialization Theory and Research.* New York: Rand McNally, 1969.

Kuhn, Thomas S. *The Structure of Scientific Revolutions.* Chicago: University of Chicago Press, 1970.

Langer, Susanne. *Philosophy in a New Key.* New York: New American Library, 1958.

Leakey, Richard E. and Roger Lewin. *People Of The Lake.* Garden City, N.Y.: Anchor Press/Doubleday, 1978.

Lee, Lee C. *Personality Development in Childhood.* Monterey, Calif.: Brooks/Cole Publishing Company, 1976.

Leff, Michael. "In Search of Ariadne's Thread: A Review of the Recent Literature on Rhetorical Theory." *Central States Speech Journal,* 1978, 29, pp. 73–91.

Lenneberg, Eric H. *Biological Foundations of Language.* New York: John Wiley and Sons, 1967.

Lentz, Tony M. "The Oral Tradition of Interpretation: Reading in Hellenic Greece as Described by Ancient Authors." Unpublished Ph.D. dissertation. University at Michigan, 1979.

Bibliography

_____. "Writing as Sophistry: From Preservation to Persuasion." *Quarterly Journal of Speech,* 1982, 68, pp. 60–68.

Liberman, A. M., F. S. Cooper, D. P. Shankweiler, and M. Studdert Kennedy. "Perception of the Speech Code." *Psychological Review,* 1967, 74, pp. 431–61.

Lieberman, Philip. *On the Origins of Language.* New York: Macmillan Publishing Company, 1975.

Linden, Eugene. *Apes, Men and Language.* New York: Saturday Review Press, 1974.

Lloyd, G. E. R. *Magic, Reason and Experience.* Cambridge: Cambridge University Press, 1979.

_____. *Polarity and Analogy.* Cambridge: Cambridge University Press, 1966.

Lord, Alfred. *The Singer of Tales.* New York: Atheneum, 1976.

Luria, A. R. *Higher Cortical Functions in Man.* New York: Basic Books, 1966.

_____. *The Human Brain and Psychologic Processes.* New York: Harper & Row, 1966.

Maher, Brendan A. "Shattered Language of Schizophrenia." In *Readings in Psychology Today.* Del Mar, Calif.: Communications/Research/Machines, 1967, 1968, 1969, pp. 377–81.

Marshack, Alexander. *The Roots of Civilization.* New York: McGraw-Hill, 1972.

McKeon, Richard. "Communication, Truth and Society." *Ethics,* 1957, 67, 2, pp. 89–99.

_____. "Discourse, Demonstration, Verification, Justification." *Logique et Analyse,* 1968, 11, pp. 37–94.

_____. "Philosophy of Communications and the Arts." in Howard E. Kiefer and Milton K. Munitz (eds.), *Perspectives in Education, Religion and the Arts.* Albany, N.Y.,: SUNY Press, 1970.

_____. "Power and the Language of Power." *Ethics.* 1958, 68, 2, pp. 98–115.

_____. (ed.) *Introduction to Aristotle.* New York: Random House, 1947.

_____. "The Uses of Rhetoric in a Technological Age: Architectonic Productive Arts." in Lloyd F. Bitzer and Edwin Black (eds.), *The Prospect of Rhetoric.* Englewood Cliffs, N.J.: Prentice-Hall, 1971.

Midgley, Mary. *Beast and Man*. New York: New American Library, 1978.

Molfese, D. L. "Cerebral Asymmetry in Infants, Children and Adults: Auditory Evoked Responses to Speech and Noise Stimuli. Unpublished Ph. D. dissertation. Pennsylvania State University, 1972.

Morse, P. A. "Infant Speech Perception: A Preliminary Model and Review of the Literature." In R. L. Schiefelbusch and L. L. Lloyd (eds.), *Language Perspectives—Acquisition, Retardation and Intervention*. Baltimore: University Park Press, 1974.

Mowrer, O. H. "The Psychologist Looks at Language." *American Psychologist,* 1954, 9, pp. 600–94.

Nauta, Walle J. H. and Michael Feirtag. "The Organization of the Brain." *Scientific American,* 1979, 241, pp. 88–111.

Osborn, Michael. "Archetypal Metaphor in Rhetoric: The Light-Dark Family." In Robert L. Scott and Bernard L. Brock, *Methods of Rhetorical Criticism*. New York: Harper & Row, 1972.

Osgood, Charles E., William H. May, and Murray S. Miron. *Cross-Cultural Universals of Affective Meaning*. Urbana: University of Illinois Press, 1975.

Osgood, C. E., G. C. Succi, and P. H. Tannenbaum. *The Measurement of Meaning*. Urbana: University of Illinois Press, 1957.

Parry, Milman. "Studies in the Epic Technique of Oral Verse-Making, I. Homer and Homeric Style." *Harvard Studies in Classical Philology.* 1930, 51, pp. 73–148.

Penfield, Wilder. *The Mystery of the Mind*. Princeton: Princeton University Press, 1975.

Perelman, Chaim. *The Idea of Justice and the Problem of Argument*. London: Routledge and Kegan Paul, 1963.

Perelman, Chaim and L. Olbrechts-Tyteca. *The New Rhetoric: A Treatise on Argumentation*. Trans. John Wilkinson and Purcell Wever. Notre Dame: University of Notre Dame Press, 1969.

Piaget, Jean. *The Child's Conception of Space*. London: Routledge & Kegan Paul, 1956.

_____. *The Construction of Reality in the Child*. New York: Basic Books, 1954.

_____. *The Origins of Intelligence in Children*. New York: Basic Books, 1954.

_____. *Play, Dreams and Imitation in Childhood*. New York: W. W. Norton, 1951.

_____. *Six Psychological Studies.* Trans. David Elkind. New York: Random House, 1967.

Pribram, Karl H. *Languages of the Brain.* Englewood Cliffs, N.J.: Prentice-Hall, 1971.

_____. "Some Comments on the Nature of the Perceived Universe." in R. E. Shaw and J. D. Bransford (eds.), *Perceiving, Acting and Knowing.* Hillsdale, N.J.: Lawrence Erlbaum Associates, 1967.

Rips, L. J., E. J. Shoben, and E. E. Smith. "Semantic Distance and the Verification of Semantic Relations." *Journal of Verbal Learning and Verbal Behavior.* 1973, 12, pp. 1–20.

Robb, Kevin. "Poetic Sources of the Greek Alphabet: Rhythm and Abecedarium from Phoenician to Greek." In Eric A. Havelock and Jackson P. Hershbell (eds.), *Communication Arts in the Ancient World* New York: Hastings House, 1978.

de Romilly, Jacqueline. *Magic and Rhetoric in Ancient Greece.* Cambridge: Harvard University Press, 1975.

Rosenberg, Bruce A. *The Art of the American Folk Preacher.* New York: Oxford University Press, 1970.

Russell, Bertrand. *Mysticism and Logic.* London: George Allen and Unwin, Ltd.

Sachs, J. S. "Recognition Memory for Syntactic and Semantic Aspects of Connected Discourse." *Perception and Psychophysics,* 1967, 2, pp. 437–42.

Schiebe, Karl E. *Mirrors, Masks, Lies and Secrets.* New York: Praeger Publishers, 1979.

Scott, Robert L. "On Viewing Rhetoric as Epistemic." *Central States Speech Journal,* 1967, 18, pp. 9–17.

_____. "On Viewing Rhetoric as Epistemic: Ten Years Later." *Central States Speech Journal,* 1976, 27, pp. 258–66.

Shaw, Robert and John Bransford (eds.). *Perceiving Acting, Knowing.* Hillsdale, N.J.: Lawrence Erlbaum Associates, 1977.

Solmsen, Friedrich. *Intellectual Experiments of the Greek Enlightenment.* Princeton: Princeton University Press, 1975.

Steel, Ronald. *Walter Lippmann and the American Century.* New York: Random House, 1980.

Steiner, George. *After Babel.* London: Oxford University Press, 1975.

Stelzner, Hermann G. " 'War Message,' December 8, 1941: An Approach to Language." In Robert L. Scott and Bernard L. Brock, *Methods of Rhetorical Criticism*. New York: Harper & Row, 1972.

Stent, Gunther S. "Cellular Communication." *Scientific American,* 1972, 227, pp. 43–51.

Stern, Daniel. *The First Relationship*. Cambridge: Harvard University Press, 1977.

Stevens, Charles F. "The Neuron." *Scientific American,* 1979, 241, pp. 54–65.

Taylor, Gordon Rattray. *The Natural History of the Mind*. New York: E. P. Dutton, 1979.

Tedlock, Dennis. "Toward an Oral Poetics." *New Literary History,* 1977, 8, pp. 507–19.

Toulmin, Stephen. *Human Understanding*. Princeton: Princeton University Press, 1977.

Turvey, Michael T. "Constructive Theory, Perceptual Systems and Tacit Knowledge." In Walter B. Weimer and David S. Palermo (eds.), *Cognition and the Symbolic Processes*. Hillsdale, N.J.: Lawrence Erlbaum Associates, 1974.

_____. "Preliminaries to a Theory of Action with Reference to Vision." In R. E. Shaw and J. D. Bransford (eds.), *Perceiving, Acting and Knowing*. Hillsdale, N.J.: Lawrence Erlbaum Associates, 1967.

Weimer, Walter B. *Notes on the Methodology of Scientific Research*. Hillsdale, N.J.: Lawrence Erlbaum Associates, 1979.

_____. "The Psychology of Inference and Expectation: Some Preliminary Remarks." In G. Maxwell and R. M. Anderson, Jr. (eds.), *Induction, Probability and Confirmation: Minnesota Studies in the Philosophy of Science, Vol. VI*. Minneapolis: University of Minnesota Press, 1975.

_____. "Science as a Rhetorical Transaction: Toward a Nonjustificational Concept of Rhetoric." *Philosophy and Rhetoric,* 1977, 10, pp. 1–29.

White, Theodore H. *The Making of the President, 1960*. New York: Atheneum, 1961.

Wilson, Edward O. *On Human Nature*. Cambridge: Harvard University Press, 1978.

Wilson, Raymond. *The Long Revolution*. London: Cox and Wyman, Pelican Books, 1965.

Wittgenstein, L. *Philosophical Investigations*. Oxford: Basil Blackwell, 1953.

Wolff, P. H. "Observations on Newborn Infants." *Psychosomatic Medicine*. 1959, 21, pp. 110–18.

Zyskind, Harold. "Some Philosophic Strands in Popular Rhetoric." In Howard E. Kiefer and Milton K. Munitz (eds.), *Perspectives in Education, Religion and the Arts*. Albany, N.Y.: SUNY Press, 1970.

INDEX

Index

Index

164

DATE DUE